Parties, Politics, and Public Policy in America

Parties, Politics, and Public Policy in America

William J. Keefe
University of Pittsburgh

HOLT, RINEHART AND WINSTON, INC.
New York   Chicago   San Francisco   Atlanta
Dallas   Montreal   Toronto   London   Sydney

To my wife and mother

Preface

The American party system is in trouble. Misunderstood by the public and flailed by critics, the party system occupies an unhappy position. Some of the criticisms directed toward the parties are close to the mark, to be sure, but others are not. Neither criticisms nor suggested reforms are likely to merit attention unless they are based on comprehending the realities of the present system. This book is addressed to the task of comprehending these realities.

It may be that the American party system needs to be rescued from its detractors, but that is not a central purpose of this book. Nor is its purpose to sketch a blueprint depicting where the best opportunities lie for reforming the parties. The purpose is rather that of exegesis: to bring into focus the salient features of the parties, to account for their form and functions, and to examine and interpret their present condition.

In a variety of ways this book attempts to illuminate a problem that is central to the American political system: the difficulties that confront the parties as governing instrumentalities. The inadequacies they sometimes reveal in meeting the task of governing, as well as in meeting other responsibilities, are not hard to understand once one knows this basic truth: The parties have been shaped more by custom than by choice, more by the environment in which they are lodged than by the decisions of political men. There are, as a result, formidable obstacles to rationalizing party structures and processes.

Although it is doubtless true that the parties have suffered from prolonged neglect by the public, the same cannot be said for the attention given them by scholars. Many excellent books and journal articles have been published on American parties, and I have drawn extensively on this literature.

This brief volume attempts to depict what we now know about this basic political institution—it is brief because, for the nonspecialist reader in particular, some things are more important to know than others. Moreover, it is worth recalling the observation of the late E. E. Schattschneider, a scholar whose work touches all who write about American politics: "The compulsion to know everything is the road to insanity." On that unassailable ground, this book leaves some lesser aspects of party unexplored, some things unsaid.

A number of people were helpful in the preparation of this manuscript. Special thanks go to friends and colleagues who read all or portions of the manuscript and made valuable suggestions: Holbert N. Carroll, Edward F. Cooke, Robert L. Donaldson, Charles O. Jones, Michael Margolis, Morris S. Ogul, and Sidney Wise. Such errors of fact and interpretation that remain in this book, as I see it, are properly theirs! The assistance of Holt, Rinehart and Winston editors and editorial staff—in particular, Herbert Addison, Jan Carr, Wyatt James, and Johnna Barto—has been much appreciated. Nancy Crockett typed portions of the manuscript and otherwise assisted this undertaking. Finally, the most important debt of all is to my wife who typed both drafts and final copy, contributed in numerous other ways, and kept me at my desk by inquiring, more times than I can count, "When are you going to finish that thing?"

W. J. K.

Pittsburgh, Pennsylvania
November 1971

Contents

ix

Tables

Figures

Parties, Politics,
and
Public Policy
in America

1
Political Parties
and the Political System

Any attempt to unravel the mysteries of American political parties might well begin with the recognition of this fact: The parties are less what they make of themselves than what their environment makes of them. The parties are not free to develop in any fashion that they might like, to take on any organizational form that might appear desirable, to pursue any course of action that might seem to be required, or to assume any responsibility that might appear appropriate. The truth of the matter is that the shape of American parties is strongly influenced by the design of the legal-political system, the election system, the political culture, and the heterogeneous quality of American life. To a remarkable extent, the party system owes its form and substance to the impact of external elements. That both the profile and substance of American parties change slowly is therefore not surprising—dramatic changes would be required outside the parties before the parties themselves would look, and perform, markedly different from the way that they do today.

The Parties and Their Environment

The Legal-Political System   No careful student of American history can escape the conclusion that the Constitution was designed by men who were suspicious of popular majorities and who had little sympathy for the functions of party. Line after line of the Constitution discloses their basic intent: to establish a government that could not easily be brought under the control of any one element, however large, that might exist within the country. The underlying philosophy of the Founding Fathers was both simple and pervasive: power was to check power, and the ambitions of some men were to check the ambitions of other men. The two main features in this design were federalism and the separation of powers—the first intended to distribute power between different levels of government; the second, to distribute power among the legislative, executive, and judicial branches. Division of the legislature into two houses, with their memberships elected for different terms and by different methods, was thought to reduce further the risk that a single faction

1

(or party) might gain ascendancy. E. E. Schattschneider has developed the argument in this fashion:

> The theory of the Constitution, inherited from the time of the Glorious Revolution in England, was legalistic and preparty in its assumptions. Great reliance was placed in a system of separation of powers, a legalistic concept of government incompatible with a satisfactory system of party government. No place was made for the parties in the system, party government was not clearly foreseen or well understood, government by parties was thought to be impossible or impracticable and was feared and regarded as something to be avoided. . . . The Convention at Philadelphia produced a constitution with a dual attitude: it was proparty in one sense and antiparty in another. The authors of the Constitution refused to suppress the parties by destroying the fundamental liberties in which parties originate. They or their immediate successors accepted amendments that guaranteed civil rights and thus established a system of party tolerance, i.e., the right to agitate and to organize. This is the proparty aspect of the system. On the other hand, the authors of the Constitution set up an elaborate division and balance of powers within an intricate governmental structure designed to make parties ineffective. It was hoped that the parties would lose and exhaust themselves in futile attempts to fight their way through the labyrinthine framework of the government, much as an attacking army is expected to spend itself against the defensive works of a fortress. This is the antiparty part of the constitutional scheme. To quote Madison, the "great object" of the Constitution was "to preserve the public good and private rights against the danger of such a faction [party] and at the same time to preserve the spirit and form of popular government."[1]

Of all the things that are inimical to the development of centralized parties, none is of greater significance than federalism. The federal scheme of organization guarantees that not only will there be fifty separate state governmental systems, but also fifty separate state party systems. No two are exactly alike. The prevailing ideology in one state party may be vastly different from that of another state party; for example, it takes no great imagination to picture the extraordinary differences that separate the state Democratic party of Mississippi from that of New York. And within each state all manner of local party organizations exist, sometimes functioning in harmony with state and national party bodies and sometimes not. Not only do the parties differ from state to state and from community to community, but the election laws that govern their activities differ. There are state laws of great variety, for example, that govern the organizational features of parties, nominating procedures, ballots, campaign finance, and elections. The thrust of federalism is thus dispersive and parochial. More than anything else, it has made the American major party an uneasy confederation of state and local parties.

---

[1] From *Party Government* by E. E. Schattschneider. Copyright 1942 by E. E. Schattschneider. Reprinted by permission of Holt, Rinehart and Winston, Inc., pp. 6–7.

The Election System   Another element in the environment of political parties is the election system. So closely linked are parties and elections that it is impossible to understand much about one without understanding a great deal about the other. Parties stay in business by winning elections. Election systems influence how the parties compete for power and the success with which they do it. Consider several examples.

Although a state's election calendar may appear neutral, even innocuous, it has a substantial bearing on party fortunes. Many state constitutions provide election calendars that separate state from national elections—for example, gubernatorial from presidential elections. The singular effect of this arrangement is to insulate state politics from national politics. The national tides that sweep one party into the presidency may be no more than ripples by the time a state election is held two years later. Although the Democratic party won presidential election after presidential election during the 1930s and 1940s, a great many governorships and state legislatures remained safely Republican, in part because of their off-year election calendars. In similar fashion, the use of staggered terms of office for legislative and executive offices diminishes the likelihood that one party can take control of both branches of government at any one time. When the governor is elected for four years and the lower house is elected for two years, prospects increase that the governor's party will lose legislative seats, and perhaps its majority, in the off-year election. The same is true in the case of the President and Congress. Whatever their virtues, staggered terms and off-year elections heighten the probability of divided control of government.

The use of single-member districts with plurality elections for the selection of legislative bodies also carries ramifications for the parties. When an election is held within a single-member district, only one party can win; the winning candidate need receive only one more vote than any other candidate, and all votes for candidates other than the victor are lost. Although the single-member district system discriminates against the second party in any district, its principal impact is virtually to rule out the possibility that a minor party can win legislative representation. Indeed, only a handful of minor party candidates have ever held seats either in Congress or in the state legislatures. The device of single-member districts with plurality elections has long been seen as one of the principal bulwarks of the *two*-party system.[2]

Few, if any, electoral arrangements apparently have had a greater impact on political parties than the direct primary, a product of the reformist movement in the early twentieth century. The primary was introduced as a means of combating the power of those party oligarchs who, shielded from popular influences, dominated state and local party conventions and chose such

[2] For a careful exposition of this argument, see Schattschneider, *Party Government*, pp. 67–84.

nominees as suited them. By contrast, the primary was designed to democratize the nominating process by empowering the voters to choose the party's nominees. Today all states employ some form of primary system, though the convention method survives for the nomination of presidential and vice-presidential candidates.

Although the precise impact of the primary on the parties is difficult to evaluate, it seems plain that its influence has been substantial. The usual arguments look like this: First, by transferring the choice of nominees from party councils to the voters, the primary has increased the probability that candidates with significantly different perspectives on public policy will be brought together in the same party. Whatever their views or policy orientations, the victors in primary elections become the party's nominees, and there is not much the party can do about it. Second, as a result, party responsibility has declined—candidates who win office largely on their own, who have their own distinctive followings within local electorates, have less reason to defer to party leaders or to follow party imperatives. Their party membership is what they choose to make it. Third, the presence of the primary has contributed to numerous intraparty clashes; particularly bitter primary fights sometimes render the party incapable of generating a united campaign in the general election. Finally, the argument has often been advanced that the primary has contributed to the spread and maintenance of one-party politics. Where one party ordinarily dominates the politics of an area, its primaries tend to become the arena where political battles are fought out. The growth of the second party is inhibited not only by the lack of voter interest in its primaries but also by its inability to attract strong candidates to its colors. One-party domination reveals little about the party's organizational strength—indeed, the prospects are high that one-party political systems will be characterized more by factionalism and internecine warfare than by unity, harmony, or ideological agreement.

Such are the arguments that have been developed against the primary. There are, of course, a number of arguments that can be made on its behalf.[3] Moreover, in some jurisdictions one or both party organizations are so powerful that "independent" candidates seldom are able to upset the "organization slate." Potential challengers may abandon their campaigns once the party organization has made known its choices. Other candidacies may never materialize because the prospects for getting the "nod" from party leaders appear so unpromising. Nevertheless, taking the country as a whole, the evidence is persuasive that the use of the primary has led to a general weakening of party organization. Unable to control its nominations, it forfeits some portion of its claim to be known as a party, some portion of its *raison*

---

[3] For a more extensive analysis of the primary, see Chapter 3, pp. 52–58.

d'être. The loose, freewheeling character of American parties owes much to the advent and consolidation of the direct primary.

To call down a further example of the relationship between the election system and the party system, one may consider the use and impact of non-partisan elections. In their search for a formula to improve city government early in the twentieth century, reformers hit upon the idea of the nonpartisan ballot—one in which party labels would not be present. The purpose of the plan was to free local government from the issues and divisiveness of national and state party politics and from the grip of local party bosses, which in turn, it was thought, would contribute to the effectiveness of local units. The nonpartisan ballot immediately gained favor and, once established, has been hard to dislodge; indeed, the plan has grown in popularity over the years. Today, well over half of the American cities with populations over 5,000 have nonpartisan elections.

A variety of political patterns hide behind the nonpartisan system. In some cities with nonpartisan ballots, such as Chicago, the party presence continues to be highly visible, and there is no doubt as to which candidates are affiliated with which parties. These elections are partisan in everything but label. In other cities local party organizations compete against slates of candidates sponsored by various nonparty groups. In still other cities the local parties are virtually without power, having lost it to interest groups that recruit, sponsor, and finance candidates for office. Finally, there are nonpartisan elections in which neither party nor nonparty groups slate candidates—thus leaving individual candidates to their own devices. The latter type is particularly prevalent among small cities.

It is difficult to say how much nonpartisan elections have diminished the vitality of local party organizations. Here and there the answer is plainly, "very little if at all"; elsewhere, the impact appears to have been substantial. Whatever the case, it is clear that where parties are shut out of the local election process, other kinds of politics enter—possibly centered around interest groups (including the press), "celebrity" or "name" politics (the latter favoring incumbents), or the idiosyncratic appeals of individual office-seekers. Where party labels are absent, power is up for grabs. Whether the voters in any real sense can hold their representatives accountable, lacking the guidance that party labels furnish, is problematical at best.[4]

Myths to the contrary, elections systems are never wholly neutral. There are election laws and constitutional arrangements that bolster the two-party system, such as the single-member district system or the rigorous require-

[4] This analysis is based principally on the research of Charles R. Adrian. See his article, "Some General Characteristics of Nonpartisan Elections," *American Political Science Review*, LXVI (September 1952), pp. 766–76, and his book, *Governing Urban America* (New York: McGraw-Hill, 1961), pp. 98–102.

ments that minor parties must meet to gain a place on the ballot, and those which make party government difficult and sometimes impossible, such as staggered terms of office, off-year elections, direct primaries, and nonpartisan ballots. The major parties, of course, are not always passive witnesses to existing electoral arrangements. At times they simply endure them because it is easier to live with customs and conventional arrangements than to try to change them or because they recognize the benefits which they confer. At other times they seek new electoral dispositions because the prospects for party advantage are sufficiently promising to warrant the effort and the risk. It is a good bet that no one understands or appreciates American election systems better than those party leaders responsible for defending party interests and winning elections.

The Political Culture and the Parties   A third important element in the environment of American political parties is the political culture—"the system of empirical beliefs, expressive symbols, and values which defines the situation in which political action takes place."[5] As commonly represented, the political culture of a nation is the amalgam of public attitudes toward the political system, its subunits, and the role of the individual within the system. It includes the knowledge and beliefs people have about the political system, their feelings toward it and their identification with it, and the evaluations that they make of it.

Although there has been little systematic research on the public's political orientations toward the party system, there is scattered evidence that large sections of the public do not perceive parties or party functions in a favorable light or approve of official behavior consonant with a theory of responsible parties.[6] An instructive study of a cross section of the Wisconsin electorate by Jack Dennis bears on these points. Table 1 shows the range of public attitudes on a series of propositions about American parties, including those which reveal diffuse or generalized support for the party system as a whole and the norm of partisanship and those which reveal acceptance of ideas or practices congruent with a system of responsible parties.

There are several conclusions to be drawn from the table. It suggests that the public regards the parties with a certain degree of ambivalence. Two items evoke a mild proparty response: 67 percent of the sample reject the proposal to remove party labels from the ballot in *all* elections—the effect of which

[5] Lucian W. Pye and Sidney Verba (eds.), *Political Culture and Political Development* (Princeton, N.J.: Princeton University Press, 1965), p. 513. See also Gabriel A. Almond and Sidney Verba, *The Civic Culture* (Boston: Little, Brown, 1963), especially pp. 1–44.

[6] A system of "responsible parties" would be characterized by centralized, unified, and disciplined parties committed to the execution of programs and promises offered at elections and held accountable by the voters for their performance.

Table 1
The Distribution of Sentiment on Items Pertaining to Support for the Party System*

ITEMS *Diffuse Support*	1 *Strongly Agree*	2 *Agree*	3 *Agree-Disagree*	4 *Disagree*	5 *Strongly Disagree*	6 *Don't Know*	7 *Not Ascertained*	*Total Percent*
The parties do more to confuse the issues than to provide a clear choice on them.	4%	50	19	20	1	5	1	100%
The party leaders make no real effort to keep their promises once they get into office.	6%	30	28	31	2	3	1	101%†
Our system of government would work a lot more efficiently if we could get rid of conflicts between the parties altogether.	9%	44	8	28	6	4	1	100%
The political parties more often than not create conflicts where none really exist.	5%	59	13	15	**	7	1	100%
It would be better if, in all elections, we put no party labels on the ballot.	3%	19	7	54	13	3	1	100%
People who work for parties during political campaigns do our nation a great service.	7%	61	19	10	**	4	**	101%†
The best rule in voting is to pick the man regardless of his party label.	23%	59	6	9	1	2	**	100%
Support for Responsible Party Government								
A senator or representative should follow his party leaders, even if he doesn't want to.	1%	22	9	56	7	4	1	100%
We would be better off if all the Democrats in government stood together and all the Republicans did the same.	2%	28	12	49	5	4	1	101%†
It is good to stick with your party through thick and thin.	3%	33	14	41	6	3	1	101%†

* Source: Jack Dennis, "Support for the Party System by the Mass Public," *American Political Science Review*, LX (September 1966), p. 605. (As adapted.)
** Less than 1%.
† Totals do not add to 100% due to rounding.

would be to institutionalize nonpartisan government—and 68 percent believe that those people who engage in campaign work for the parties perform a valuable function. On all other counts, negative feelings toward the parties predominate. A clear majority of the public believes that the parties do more to confuse issues than to clarify them, that government would perform better without conflict between the parties, and that the parties create unnecessary conflicts. Only 10 percent disagree with the proposition that "the best rule in voting is to pick the man regardless of his party label."

Of equal interest, the study reveals that support for cohesive and disciplined parties is relatively meager. Less than a quarter of the respondents agree on the key proposition that "a senator or representative should follow his party leaders, even if he doesn't want to." A slightly larger percentage agrees to a variant of the first item—that "we would be better off if all Democrats in government stood together and all the Republicans did the same." Overall, there is little in this profile of popular attitudes that portends public understanding or acceptance of the tenets of a responsible party system.

Further analysis of the data according to the education of the respondents and the intensity of their party identification yields additional insights into the character of party support. Interestingly, individuals with higher educational attainments score higher on the diffuse support dimension than those with lesser education, and those with lesser education are more inclined to accept the norms of responsible parties than those with higher education. The more favorable attitudes of better educated citizens may result from the fact that, as a rule, they are more active in politics, more politically aware, and perceive a greater stake in preserving existing institutions. Individuals with strong party identification are more likely to hold favorable attitudes toward the parties and toward the idea of responsible parties than those who are moderate partisans or independents. Strong Democrats in particular see merit in disciplined, cohesive parties. For the general population, however, there is slight enthusiasm for reform of the party system that would alter their decentralized, freewheeling, and heterogeneous character. Whatever else may be said, the public prefers some version of a loose and unstructured party system, and even this, it appears, is accepted grudgingly.[7]

Generalizing about national patterns from the data gathered in one state is risky. Nevertheless, it appears likely in this case that the orientations of the Wisconsin voters to the parties is fairly representative of the nation as a whole. Although a strong majority of people vote within the framework of their party affiliations, their interest in parties often stops at that point. A recent nation-wide survey of voter attitudes toward control of the presidency and Congress by the same party, shown in Table 2, helps to fill out the argu-

---

[7] The data and general line of argument developed in these paragraphs are derived from Jack Dennis, "Support for the Party System by the Mass Public," *American Political Science Review*, LX (September 1966), pp. 600–615.

Table 2
Voter Attitudes Toward Party Control of Government*

Do you feel it is better to have a President and a Congress controlled by the same political party, or is it better to have the President of one party and Congress controlled by another party, or doesn't it make much difference?

President and Congress of Same or Different Parties?

	Total Voters %
Both same party	36
Different parties better	32
Not much difference	24
Not sure	8
	100%

* Source: Louis Harris Survey Report, March 9, 1970.

ment. Only slightly more than one-third (36 percent) of the people believe it is preferable to have the President's party holding a majority in Congress. Approximately two-thirds (64 percent) of the voters prefer that different parties control the branches, believe it doesn't make much difference whether there is division or not, or are uncertain as to what is best. It seems clear from these data that most American voters are dubious of government by party.

The evidence of these pages is that American political parties rest on a relatively narrow and uncertain base of popular support. Scarcely anyone can fail to notice the widespread skepticism of politics and politicians that pervades popular thought. Few vocations stir so little interest as that of the politician. The language of American politics is itself laced with suspicion and hostility. In the argot of popular appraisal, political organizations turn into "machines," party workers emerge as "hacks," political leaders become "bosses," and campaign appeals degenerate into "empty promises" or "sheer demagoguery." The fact that some politicians have contributed to this state of affairs, by debasing the language of political discourse or by their behavior, is perhaps beside the point. The critical fact is that the American political culture contains a strong suspicion of the political process and the agencies that ordinarily dominate it, the political parties. Though it is difficult to evaluate in any precise way, there is little doubt that the skepticism that pervades popular thought about the parties contributes to their devitalization as organizations.

A Heterogeneous Nation To complete the analysis of the environment of American parties, it is necessary to say something about the characteristics of the nation as a whole. No array of statistics is required to make the point that in the magnitude of its diversity, no nation can lay greater claim than the United States. The American community is composed of an endless variety of economic and social interests, class configurations, ethnic and religious groups, occupations, regional and subregional interests and loyalties, values, and beliefs. There are citizens who are deeply attached to inherited patterns and those who are impatient advocates of change, those who care intensely about politics and those who can take it or leave it, and those who elude labeling—those who are active on one occasion and passive on another. There are citizens who think mainly in terms of farm policy, some who seek advantage for urban elements, others whose lives and political interests revolve around businesses or professions. Diversity abounds. Sometimes deep, sometimes shallow, the differences that separate one group from another and one region from another make the formation of public policy that suits everyone all but impossible.

The essential requirement for any major party is that it be able to accommodate itself to the vast diversity that lies within the nation. The result has been the emergence of major parties that, by and large, are remarkably hospitable to all points of view and to all manner of interests and people. From one point of view they are loose and untidy systems characterized more by their coalition quality than by unity. Herbert Agar makes the case succinctly:

> Most politics will be parochial, most politicians will have small horizons, seeking the good of the state or the district rather than of the Union; yet by diplomacy and compromise, never by force, the government must water down the selfish demands of regions, races, classes, business associations, into a national policy which will alienate no major groups and which will contain at least a plum for everybody. This is the price of unity in a continentwide federation.[8]

Party Organization

Regardless of variations in emphasis, there are two features that are common to party organizations throughout the United States. First, parties are organized in a series of committees, extending from the precinct level to the national committee. And second, party committee organization has been developed to parallel the arrangement of electoral districts. With the exception of heavily one-party areas, party committees of some type will be found in almost all jurisdictions within which government officials of importance are elected.

A familiar description of American parties begins by likening their organizational structure to that of a pyramid. At the top of the pyramid rests the

---

[8] Herbert Agar, *The Price of Union* (Boston: Houghton Mifflin, 1950), p. xiv.

national committee, at the bottom the precinct organizations, with various ward, city, county, and state committees lodged in between. Although it is convenient to view party organization within this pattern, it is misleading if it suggests that power flows from top to bottom, from major national leaders to local rank-and-file. Nothing could be further from the truth, for committees at each level have substantial autonomy, and, moreover, power is more likely to be discovered at the state and local levels than anywhere else.

The National Committee   The most prestigious and visible of all party committees is the national committee.[9] In the Democratic party its membership consists of a committeeman and committeewoman for each of the fifty states. In addition to providing two-member representation from each state, the Republican party awards a third seat to each state that in the last election cast its electoral votes for the Republican presidential candidate, elected a Republican governor, or captured a majority of the state's congressional delegation. National committeemen and women are chosen in a variety of ways in the states, with their official tenure beginning once they are accepted by the national convention of the party.

To know what the national committee is, it is necessary to look at what it does. By and large, its activities are not impressive. One of its principal responsibilities is to make arrangements for the national convention every four years. In this capacity it chooses the convention site, prepares a temporary roster of convention delegates, and selects convention speakers and temporary officers who will manage the assembly in its opening phase. The committee is especially active during presidential campaigns in coordinating campaign efforts, publicizing the party and its candidates, and raising money. Following the election, the committee often faces the task of raising the necessary funds to pay off campaign debts.

The national committees come to life during presidential election years, for their major efforts are directed toward the election of their party's presidential candidate. During nonpresidential years most of the national committee's work is carried on by committees or the national chairman. Study groups occasionally are created by the committee (perhaps under instructions from the national convention) to examine certain problems such as party organization, party policy, or convention management. In 1969, for example, the Democratic National Committee created the Commission on Party Structure and Delegate Selection to hold hearings and to suggest proposals for changes in party procedures. Included in its wide-ranging report were recommendations urging state parties (and state legislatures) to eliminate discrimination

---

[9] For an instructive study of the national committee and the national chairman, see Cornelius P. Cotter and Bernard C. Hennessy, *Politics Without Power: The National Party Committees* (New York: Atherton Press, 1964).

of all kinds in party rules, to open party meetings and processes to participation by all members of the party, to remove or moderate restrictive voter registration laws or practices, to apportion convention delegates within states in a manner that would give equitable representation to areas of Democratic strength, and to provide for fair representation of minority political views in the selection of delegates to the national convention. Laced with controversy, the Commission's agenda for reform seemed certain to occupy the party's attention for years to come.

The National Chairman   The head of the national party is the national chairman.[10] Although the chairman is officially selected by the members of the national committee, in practice he is chosen by the party's presidential candidate shortly after the national convention has adjourned. Very few chairmen in either party have held the position for an extended period of time—the chairman of the party winning the presidency usually receives a major appointment in the new administration, and the chairman of the losing party is replaced by a new face. When a vacancy in the chairmanship of the "out" party occurs, selection of the new chairman is made by the national committee. Factional conflicts may come to the surface when the committee is faced with the responsibility of finding a replacement, since the leading candidates will invariably be identified with certain wings of the party.

The central problem with which the national chairman must come to terms in presidential election years is the direction and coordination of the national campaign. The chairman has few powers but important responsibilities. In raising presidential campaign funds, he competes with other campaign managers and party units for scarce resources; in seeking to focus attention on the presidential campaign, he competes with other politicos concerned with other campaigns; in seeking to unify the party, he is often thwarted by party elements whose interests run counter to his and those of the presidential candidate; in attempting to influence and publicize national party policies, he collides with the nagging realities of parochialism, sectionalism, and indifference. Apart from the prestige that attaches to the office, there are few rewards that flow regularly to the national chairman. He holds a job without much security, heads a committee without real powers, and speaks for a party for whom in fact no one person can speak.

Congressional and Senatorial Campaign Committees   The other principal units of the national party organization are the congressional and senatorial campaign committees, one for each party in each house. These committees,

[10] See Cotter and Hennessy, *Politics without Power*, pp. 67–80. They see the roles of the national chairman as "image-maker, hell-raiser, fund-raiser, campaign manager, and administrator."

composed of members of Congress, are wholly independent of the national committees. The campaign committees are an outgrowth of the need of members of Congress to have organizations concerned exclusively with their political welfare. As such, they raise campaign funds for members, help to develop campaign strategies, conduct research, and otherwise provide assistance to members running for reelection. In addition, the committees make available limited funds for party candidates in states or districts where the party has no incumbent. A certain degree of informal cooperation takes place between the party committees of Congress and the national committees, but for the most part they go their separate ways, one preoccupied with the presidential race, the others bent on securing reelection of incumbent legislators and on improving the party's prospects for winning or retaining control of Congress. Independent, self-reliant, suspicious, absorbed in a narrow range of party interests, they run true to form as American party committees.

State Committees   Midway between the national party apparatus and local party organizations are the state party committees, often called state central committees. So great are the differences between these committees from state to state—in membership selection, size, and function—that it is difficult to generalize about them. In some states the membership is made up of county chairmen; more commonly, state committeemen and women are chosen in primaries or by local party conventions. Their size ranges from less than a hundred members to several hundred. There are states in which the state central committee is a genuinely powerful party unit and is charged by custom with drafting the party platform, slating statewide candidates, and waging an intensive fund-raising campaign. In other states the committee's impact on state politics is scarcely perceptible. In a fashion similar to that found at the national level, the state chairman is ordinarily selected by the party's gubernatorial candidate. And like the national chairman, the state chairman is usually a key adviser to the governor on party affairs, particularly on matters involving the distribution of patronage.

Local Party Organization   Below the state committee of the party is the county committee, ordinarily a very large organization composed of all the precinct officials within the county. At the head of this committee is the county chairman, who is usually elected by the members of the county committee. Often a key figure in local party organization, the county chairman is active in the campaign planning, in the recruitment and slating of party candidates, in the supervision of campaign financing, and in the allocation of patronage to the party faithful. In many counties the county chairman's power is enhanced by the fact that he actively recruits candidates for precinct committeemen and committeewomen—the very people who in turn elect him to office.

In some states there are congressional district party organizations, developed around the office of congressman. Where these committees exist, they function essentially as the congressman's personal organization, set off from the rest of the party and preoccupied with "errand running" for constituents and the election of the congressman. Although local party officials, such as the county chairman, may be instrumental in controlling the original congressional nomination, their influence on the congressman's policy orientations is virtually nil. Indeed, one of the dominant characteristics of congressional district organization is its autonomy.[11] Further down the line are the city and ward committees, which vary in size and importance throughout the country. Their activities, like those of other committees, are centered around campaigns and elections.

The cornerstone of American party organization is the precinct committee, organized within the tens of thousands of election or voting districts of the nation. In metropolitan areas a precinct is likely to number one or two thousand voters, while in open-country areas, perhaps only a dozen. The complexity of party organization at the precinct level is mainly a function of precinct size. The precinct committeeman and/or committeewoman is chosen in one of two ways: by the voters in a primary election or by the vote of party members attending a precinct caucus.

In the lore of American politics, elections are won or lost at the precinct level. A strong precinct organization, the argument runs, is essential to party victory, and the key to a strong organization is a precinct leader bent on carrying his precinct. In attempting to advance his party's fortunes, the committeeman engages in four main activities: those associated with the campaign itself, party organizational work (for example, recruitment and organization of workers), promulgation of political information, and identification and recruitment of candidates for local office. For most jurisdictions, it appears, his most important activities are those related to the campaign, such as inducing and helping people to register, contacting voters, raising money, campaigning for votes, and transporting voters to the polls. Undoubtedly there are differences in the role perceptions of party officials. A study of precinct leaders in Massachusetts and North Carolina, for example, found that about 60 percent saw their principal task as that of mobilizing voters.[12] In the Detroit metropolitan area, by contrast, less than half (45 percent) evaluated their primary task as the production of votes; surprisingly large numbers in this sample (24 percent) defined their role as that of "ideological mentor" —that is, charged with the responsibility of educating voters concerning government and public issues; and others (18 percent) defined their role as

[11] See Avery Leiserson, "National Party Organization and Congressional Districts," *Western Political Quarterly*, XVI (September 1963), pp. 633–649.

[12] Lewis Bowman and G. R. Boynton, "Activities and Role Definitions of Grassroots Party Officials," *Journal of Politics*, XXVIII (February 1966), pp. 121–143.

that of promoting social and economic welfare efforts.[13] Whether variations in the role perceptions of precinct officials have an important bearing on party efforts to win elections is difficult to say. There is very little systematic evidence concerning the components present in winning elections or, for that matter, in losing them.

Extraparty Groups In a few states and localities the most important party agencies are not the formal party organizations but rather extralegal associations formed by party members to accomplish various purposes. These unofficial organizations come in all sizes and shapes. Some were formed in order to wrest political power away from the regular party organizations, while others were formed as a means of fostering greater concern with issues in state and local politics. Among the most prominent examples of these associations are the California Republican Assembly, the California Democratic Council, the voluntary associations in both parties in Wisconsin, and the Democratic reform clubs of New York City. Composed of dues-paying, well-educated, mainly middle-class members, these organizations have at times been more effective than the regular organizations in California and Wisconsin; indeed, the party national committees have sometimes dealt with these associations rather than the official organizations.[14] The political clubs differ sharply from "old-style" political organizations in their lack of interest in patronage, their preoccupation with public policy and ideological problems, and the professional-business-university backgrounds of their members. The best measure of their power in state politics, particularly in California and Wisconsin, has been their substantial success in controlling the party's nominating process through the practice of slating candidates in advance of the primaries.[15]

In addition to the extralegal party groups noted above, which both complement and compete with the regular organizations, there are a host of auxiliary organizations that spring up during campaigns. Presidential campaigns are replete with groups such as Independents for Nixon, Lawyers for Humphrey, Citizens for Eisenhower, Volunteers for Stevenson, and Businessmen for Kennedy. In some cases closely linked to the formal party apparatus and in other cases largely independent, these groups raise and spend money, develop campaign plans, and solicit votes. One appeal of these groups is that they permit

[13] Samuel J. Eldersveld, *Political Parties: A Behavioral Analysis,* © 1964 by Rand McNally & Company, Chicago, pp. 253–254.

[14] See Hugh A. Bone, *American Politics and the Party System* (New York: McGraw-Hill, 1971), pp. 139–141.

[15] For comprehensive studies of these new-style political organizations, see Frank J. Sorauf, "Extra-Legal Parties in Wisconsin," *American Political Science Review,* XLVIII (September 1954), James Q. Wilson, *The Amateur Democrats* (Chicago: University of Chicago Press, 1962), and Francis Carney, *The Rise of the Democratic Clubs in California* (New York: McGraw-Hill, 1960).

citizens who are reluctant to be identified with the formal party organizations to play a role in campaigns. From the party's perspective, these organizations provide additional sources of campaign money and political workers, not to mention an added measure of legitimacy for its candidates. There are, finally, the youth groups in the party organizations, the Young Democrats and the Young Republicans—in some communities highly active in politics, elsewhere essentially social organizations.

The Changing Parties: "Old-Style" and "New-Style" Politics   In the late nineteenth century and early twentieth century the best examples of strong party organization could be found in the large cities of the Northeast and Midwest—New York City, Boston, Philadelphia, Jersey City, Kansas City, and Chicago. Well-organized and strongly disciplined, the urban "machine" during this era was well-nigh invincible. Precinct and ward officials maintained steady contacts with their party constituencies, finding jobs for people out of work, helping those who were in trouble with the law, helping others to secure government benefits such as welfare assistance, assisting neighborhoods to secure government services, helping immigrants to cope with a new society, and facilitating merchants and tradespeople in their efforts to obtain contracts, licenses, and the like. The party organization was at the center of community life, an effective mediary between the people and their government. Party officials were "brokers," exchanging information, access, and influence for loyalty and support at the polls.

Today the picture has changed. Although the parties continue to perform many social services in the larger cities, taken as a whole the volume of such exchanges is far below that of the past. A number of factors have brought this about, including the growth of civil service systems and the corresponding decline in patronage, the relative decline in the value of patronage jobs,[16] the arrival of the "welfare state" with its various benefits for low-income groups, the steady assimilation of immigrants, the growing disillusionment among better educated voters over many features of "machine" politics, and the coming of age of the mass media with its potential for contacts between candidates and their publics. There remain, of course, many disadvantaged citizens, particularly in large cities, who continue to rely on local party leaders for assistance in solving the problems in their lives. But most Americans scarcely give a thought to using party officials in this way. Where the parties have suffered a loss of functions, it is reasonable to assume that they have also

[16] For an examination of party patronage and its limitations, see Frank J. Sorauf, "State Patronage in a Rural County," *American Political Science Review*, L (December 1956), pp. 1046–1056, and "Patronage and Party," *Midwest Journal of Political Science*, III (May 1959), pp. 115–126. See also Daniel P. Moynihan and James Q. Wilson, "Patronage in New York State, 1955–1959," *American Political Science Review*, LVIII (June 1964), pp. 286–301.

suffered a loss of vitality. The result, undoubtedly, has been a decline in their ability to "deliver the vote" on election day.

Although it is clear that the "old-style" politics of the cities—with its emphasis on strong leadership, disciplined cadres of party workers, patronage, and services for party voters—is no longer as important as it once was, it is still much too early to announce its demise. One indication of this may be found in the extent to which party officials continue to perform the voter-servicing functions traditionally associated with party organizations. Table 3, reporting the findings for a sample of Democratic and Republican party leaders in New Jersey, indicates that those activities designed to assist the party in mobilizing votes are by no means out of style.

Despite the vitality of party organizations here and there, it is apparent that the "new politics" of the 1950s and 1960s has changed familiar political terrain. Today there are far more amateur activists in political campaigns than ever before. Youthful, suspicious of party "machines," repelled by patronage and "deals," committed to opening up the political process, and most important, engrossed in the analysis and development of issues, the new class of reformers has had a dramatic effect on American politics. No better example could be found than the legions of young activists—mainly college and university students—who fanned out across the country during the 1968 Democratic presidential primaries to campaign on behalf of Senator Eugene McCarthy of Minnesota. Two years later these and other amateurs again took to the hustings to work for the election of "peace" candidates in the 1970 congressional elections. The long-run significance for the parties of this new breed of activist is problematical. Reform movements are more difficult to sustain than to launch. For purposes of this analysis, however, the most interesting aspect of the arrival of the amateurs in politics may lie in their approach to campaigning. Borrowing heavily from the copybooks of established party organizations, their essential strategy has been to meet the voters on their home grounds, in much the same way that active party workers have always done. "If the new politics teaches anything," one powerful Democratic county leader in New York has said, "it's that the old politics was pretty good. The McCarthy kids in New Hampshire rang doorbells, made the telephone calls, made the personal contact that people associate with the old-style machine."[17]

[17] Martin Tolchin, "Democratic 'Bosses': Mechanics of Power," *The New York Times* (June 1, 1970), p. 27. For an account of a big city party organization that continues to be extraordinarily powerful (the Daley Organization in Chicago), see Andrew M. Greeley, "Take Heart from the Heartland," *The New Republic* (December 12, 1970), pp. 12–19. The essence of "machine" politics in Chicago is reflected in the comment of a black political leader: "We're loyal to the organization because it works, because we know of no better way of improving our position in Chicago, and because, while it can't give everyone everything he wants, it can give most Chicago groups enough to keep them happy." Reprinted by permission of *The New Republic*, © 1970, Harrison-Blaine of New Jersey, Inc., p. 17.

Table 3

Percentage of Leaders Who Said They Performed
Various Tasks to Help the People in Their Area*

Task	Performed Often (a)	Performed Once in a While (b)	(a+b)	Never Performed
Helping poorer people get work	72%	26%	98%	2%
Helping deserving people get public jobs on a highway crew, in the fire department or police force, or in state positions	72	22	94	6
Showing people how to get their social security benefits, welfare, unemployment compensation, and so forth	59	30	89	11
Helping citizens with problems like rent gouging, unfair labor practices, zoning, or unfair assessments	54	30	84	16
Helping your part of town or some other political leader to get a needed traffic light, more parking space, more policemen, and so forth	60	23	83	17
Running clambakes and other get-togethers for interested people even though no campaign is on	45	36	81	19
Helping citizens who are in difficulty with the law. Do you help them get straightened out?	62	17	79	21

* Source: Richard T. Frost, "Stability and Change in Local Party Politics," *Public Opinion Quarterly*, XXV (Summer 1961), pp. 221–235.

The Activities of Parties

Among the principal thrusts of scholarship on political parties is the thesis that political parties are indispensable instruments in the functioning of democratic political systems. Scholars have differed sharply in their approaches to the study of parties and in their appraisals of the functions or activities of parties, but they are in striking agreement as to the linkage between parties and democracy. Representative of a wide band of analysis, the following statements by V. O. Key, Jr., and E. E. Schattschneider sketch the broad outlines of the argument:

> Governments operated, of course, long before political parties in the modern sense came into existence. . . . The proclamation of the right of men to have a hand in their own governing did not create institutions by which they might exercise that right. Nor did the machinery of popular government come into existence overnight. By a tortuous process party systems came into being to implement democratic ideas. As democratic ideas corroded the old foundations of authority, members of the old governing elite reached out to legitimize their positions under the new notions by appealing for popular support. That appeal compelled deference to popular views, but it also required the development of organization to communicate with and to manage the electorate. . . . In a sense, government, left suspended in mid-air by the erosion of the old justifications for its authority, had to build new foundations in the new environment of a democratic ideology. In short, it had to have machinery to win votes.[18]

> The rise of political parties is indubitably one of the principal distinguishing marks of modern government. The parties, in fact, have played a major role as *makers* of governments, more especially they have been the makers of democratic government. . . . [Political] parties created democracy and . . . modern democracy is unthinkable save in terms of the parties. . . . The parties are not . . . merely appendages of modern government; they are in the center of it and play a determinative and creative role in it.[19]

The contributions of political parties to the maintenance of democratic politics can be judged in a rough way by examining the principal activities in which they engage. Of particular importance are those activities associated with the recruitment and selection of leadership, the representation and integration of interests, and the control and direction of government.

Recruitment and Selection of Leaders The processes by which political leaders are recruited, elected, and appointed to office form the central core of party activity.[20] Except where authentic nonpartisan elections exist, political

---

[18] V. O. Key, Jr., *Politics, Parties, & Pressure Groups* (New York: Crowell, 1964), pp. 200–201.

[19] From *Party Government* by E. E. Schattschneider. Copyright 1942 by E. E. Schattschneider. Reprinted by permission of Holt, Rinehart and Winston, Inc., p. 1.

[20] Agreement among students of political parties as to the nature of party functions, their relative significance, and the consequences of functional performance for the political system is far from complete. Frank J. Sorauf points out that among the functions that have been attributed to American parties have been those of simplifying political issues and alternatives, producing automatic majorities, recruiting political leadership and personnel, organizing minorities and opposition, moderating and compromising political conflict, organizing the machinery of government, promoting political consensus and legitimacy, and bridging the separation of powers. The principal difficulty with listings of this sort, according to Sorauf, is that "it involves making functional statements about

parties are the dominant agencies for identifying potential officeholders, sorting them out, channeling them into candidacies, and mobilizing the voters necessary to their election. The party interest, moreover, extends to the appointment of administrative and judicial officers—for example, cabinet members, justices of the Supreme Court—once the party has captured the executive branch of government.[21] As noted earlier, the party *organizations* do not everywhere dominate the process by which candidates are either recruited or nominated. Some candidates are "self-starters," choosing to enter primaries without waiting for approval from party chieftains. With their own personal followings and sources of financial support, they may pay scant heed to party leaders or party policies. Other candidates are plainly recruited, groomed, and financed by political interest groups. The looseness of the American party system, due largely to the primary, creates conditions under which party control over some of the candidates who run under its banner is thin or nonexistent.

Still and all, the political parties play a massive role in generating candidates and electing them to office. It is difficult to see how hundreds of thousands of elective offices could be filled in the absence of parties without turning each election into a free-for-all, conspicuous by the presence of numerous candidates holding all varieties of set, shifting, and undisclosed views. Forming a government out of such an odd mélange of officials would be next to impossible. Collective accountability to the voters would disappear. Whatever their shortcomings, by proposing alternative lists of candidates and campaigning on their behalf the parties bring important measures of order, routine, and predictability to the electoral process.

The constant factors in party politics are the pursuit of power, office, and

---

party activity without necessarily relating them to functional requisites or needs of the system." He suggests that at this stage of research on parties emphasis should be given to the activities performed by parties, thus avoiding the confusion arising from the lack of clarity about the meaning of function, the absence of consensus on functional categories, and the problem of measuring the performance of functions. See his instructive essay, "Political Parties and Political Analysis," in William Nisbet Chambers and Walter Dean Burnham (eds.), *The American Party Systems: Stages of Political Development* (New York: Oxford, 1967), pp. 33–53.

[21] In about four-fifths of the states, judges are chosen in some form of partisan or nonpartisan election. In the remaining states they come to office through appointment. A few states employ the so-called Missouri Plan of judge selection, under which the governor makes judicial appointments from a list of names supplied by a nonpartisan judicial commission composed of judges, lawyers, and laymen. Under this plan, designed to take judges "out of politics," each judge, after a trial period, runs for re-election without opposition; voters may vote either to retain or to remove him from office. If a majority of the voters cast affirmative ballots, the judge is continued in office for a full term, and if the vote is negative, the judge loses office and the governor makes another appointment in the same manner. Even under this plan, of course, the governor may give preference to aspirants of his own party. The truth of the matter is that irrespective of the system used to choose judges, party leaders and party interest will nearly always be involved.

advantage. Yet in serving their own interest of winning office, parties make other contributions to the public at large and to the political system. Among other things, they help to educate the voters concerning issues and mobilize them for political action, provide a linkage between the people and the government, and simplify the choices to be made in elections. The parties do what voters cannot do by themselves: from the totality of interests and issues in politics, they choose those that will become "the agenda of formal public discourse."[22] In the process of shaping the agenda, they provide a mechanism by which voters can not only make sense out of what government does, but also relate to the government itself. The role of the parties in educating voters and in structuring opinion has been described by Robert MacIver in this way:

> Public opinion is too variant and dispersive to be effective unless it is organized. It must be canalized on the broad lines of some major division of opinion. Party focuses the issues, sharpens the differences between contending sides, eliminates confusing cross-currents of opinion. . . . The party educates the public while seeking merely to influence it, for it must appeal on grounds of policy. For the same reason it helps to remove the inertia of the public and thus to broaden the range of public opinion. In short the party, in its endeavors to win the public to its side, however unscrupulous it may be in its modes of appeal, is making the democratic system workable. It is the agency by which public opinion is translated into public policy.[23]

Representation and Integration of Group Interests The American nation is extraordinarily complex and heterogeneous. All kinds of political interest groups exist within its borders. Given the diversity in the objectives of different groups, conflict inevitably arises between one group and another and between various groups and the government. To a notable extent the parties keep conflict of this sort within tolerable limits. Relations between the parties and private organizations take on the character of a marriage of convenience —groups need the parties as much as the parties need them. No group can expect to move far toward the attainment of its objectives without coming to terms with the realities of party power; the parties, after all, are in a strategic position to advance or retard the objectives of any group. Similarly, no party can expect to achieve broad electoral successes without a firm base of group support.

In one sense the parties serve as "brokers" among the organized interests of American society, weighing the claims of one group against those of another, accepting some programs, and modifying or rejecting others. The steady bargaining that occurs between interest groups and the parties (both

[22] Theodore J. Lowi, "Party, Policy, and Constitution in America," in William Nisbet Chambers and Walter Dean Burnham (eds.) *The American Party Systems,* p. 263.
[23] Robert MacIver, *The Web of Government* (New York: Macmillan, 1947), p. 213.

in and out of government) tends to produce settlements to which the participants can accommodate for a time, even though they may not be wholly
satisfactory to any one. The processes of bargaining and compromise are
essential elements in the strategy of American parties. Moreover, the legitimacy of the government itself is likely to depend on the capacity of the parties
to represent diverse interests and to integrate the claims of competing groups
in a broad program of public policy.

The thesis that the major parties are steadily sensitive to the representation
of group interests cannot be advanced without a caveat or two. The stubborn
fact is that the parties are far more solicitous toward the claims of organized
interests than toward those of unorganized interests. The groups that regularly
engage the attention of the parties and their representatives in government are
those whose support (or opposition) can make a difference at the polls.
Organized labor, organized business, organized agriculture, organized medi-
cine—all have multiple channels for gaining access to decision-makers.
Indeed, party politicians are about as likely to search out the views of these
interests as to wait to hear from them. By contrast, many millions of Americans are all but shut out of the political system. The political power of such
groups as agricultural workers, sharecroppers, migrants, and unorganized
labor has never been commensurate with their numbers or, for that matter,
with their contribution to society. With low participation in elections, weak
organizations, low status, and poor access to political communications, their
voices are often drowned out in the din produced by organized interests.

No problem of representation in America is more important than that of
finding ways by which to move the claims of the unorganized public onto
the agenda of politics. But the task is formidable: "All power is organization
and all organization is power. . . . A man who has no share in any form of
organized power is not independent of organized power. He is at the mercy
of it. . . ."[24]

Control and Direction of Government   A third major activity of the parties
involves the control and direction of government. Parties recruit candidates
and organize campaigns in order to win political power, gain public office, and
take control of government. Given the character of the political system and
the parties themselves, it is unrealistic to suppose that party management of
government will be altogether successful. In the first place, the separate
branches of government may not be captured by the same party. Only one-
half of the elections since 1950, for example, have resulted in control of both
houses of Congress and the presidency by the same party. Division of party
control complicates the process of governing, forcing the President not only to

[24] Harvey Fergusson, *People and Power* (New York: Morrow, 1947), pp. 101–102.

work with his own party in Congress but also with elements of the other party. Party achievements in majority-building tend to be blurred in the mix of coalition votes, and party accountability to the voters suffers. In the second place, even though one party may organize both the legislative and the executive branches, there is a good possibility that its margin of seats in the legislature will be too thin to permit it to govern effectively. Moreover, internal disagreement within the majority party may be so great on certain kinds of issues that it is virtually impossible for it to pull its ranks together and to develop coherent positions. When majority party lines are shattered, opportunities come into view for the minority party to assert itself forcefully in the policy-making process. Overall, what has been said about the problem of the majority party in managing the government at the national level applies in about the same fashion to most state governments.

The upshot of this is that although the parties organize governments, they do not completely dominate their decision-making activities. In some measure they compete with political interest groups bent on securing public policies advantageous to their clienteles, and there are times when certain groups have fully as much influence on the behavior of legislators and bureaucrats as legislative party leaders, national and subnational party leaders, or the President. Yet to point out the difficulties that confront the parties in seeking to manage the government is not to suggest that the parties' impact on public policy is insubstantial. Not even a casual examination of party platforms, candidates' and officeholders' speeches, or legislative voting can fail to detect the contributions of the parties to shaping the direction of government or, in fact, ignore the differences that separate the parties on public policy matters.[25]

One begins to understand American parties by recognizing that party politicians are more likely to set great store in the notion of winning elections than in using election outcomes to achieve a broad range of policy goals. To be sure, they have interests and commitments in policy questions but rarely to the point that rules out bargaining and compromise in the interest of achieving half a "party loaf." Politicians tend to be intensely pragmatic and adaptable men. For the most part, they are attracted to a particular party more because of its promise as a mechanism for moving into government than as a mechanism for governing itself. It is not surprising, then, that the electoral party organization is more highly developed than the party apparatus in government—that office-filling tasks take on more importance than policy-shaping or policy-making. Party is a way of organizing activists and supporters

---

[25] For an examination of the policy differences between the parties in recent Congresses, see Chapter 5, especially pp. 115–123. For a study that reveals the importance of party platforms in the national policy-making process, see Paul T. David, "Party Platforms as National Plans," *Public Administration Review*, XXXI (May–June 1971), pp. 303–315.

in order to make a bid for office.[26] This is the elemental truth of party politics. That the election of one aggregation of politicians as against another aggregation of politicians has policy significance, as indeed it does, comes closer to representing an unanticipated dividend than a triumph for the idea of responsible party government.

[26] Party may be conceptualized in a number of ways. See an analysis of various concepts of party, as well as the functions of party, in Anthony King, "Political Parties in Western Democracies," *Polity* (Winter 1969), pp. 111–141.

2
The Characteristics of American Parties

The major parties are firm landmarks on the American political scene. In existence in their present form for over a century, the major parties have made important contributions to the development and maintenance of a democratic political culture and democratic institutions and practices. In essence, the parties form the principal institution for popular control of government, and this achievement is all the more remarkable for the limitations under which they function. This chapter examines the principal characteristics of the American party system.

The Primary Characteristic: Decentralization

There is no lively debate among political scientists concerning the dominant characteristic of American political parties. It is, pure and simple, their decentralization. Viewed at some distance, party organization may appear to be neatly ordered and hierarchical—committees are piled, one atop another, from the precinct level to the national committee, conveying the impression that power flows from the top to the bottom. In point of fact, however, the American party is but a pale imitation of hierarchical organization. The power of national party instrumentalities over state and local organizations is thin and insubstantial. The rules that state and local organizations adopt, the candidates they recruit or help to recruit, the money they raise, the innovations they introduce, the policy orientations they develop—all bear the distinctive imprints of local and state leaders and the interests they represent. To be sure, national party officials often monitor carefully the activities of state and local organizations, but that is nearly always the extent of their involvement.

Weak National Parties   No elaborate argument is needed to establish the point concerning the organizational decentralization of American parties. Evidence is everywhere available that national party agencies cannot dominate state and local party leaders. Should national party leaders seek to influence the nomination of candidates for Congress, for example, the prospects are that they would be met by rebuff and defeat. Although the President obviously has a stake in the policy orientations of candidates his party recruits for Congress—since his legislative program will come before them—there is little he can do to shape the decisions of local party chieftains or electorates. Custom dictates that he follow a "hands-off" policy in the choice of congressional candidates.[1] Moreover, it is exceedingly rare for party leaders in Congress to attempt to discipline fellow party members who stray off the reservation, voting with the other party on key legislative issues or otherwise failing to come to the aid of their party.[2] Congressmen who neglect or demean their party not only escape sanctions but also, by dramatizing their capacity to resist party pressures, may improve their fortunes with the voters back home —such is the case in a loose and decentralized party system.

Finally, the essential weakness of the national party apparatus is revealed in the character and activities of the national committee of each party. Nominally located at the summit of the party hierarchy, the committee's roots are actually buried in the states; although committee members are formally elected by the party's national convention every four years, in reality the convention merely accepts the nominees put forward by the state delegations. Moreover, in no important sense can the national committee speak for the party. It meets infrequently and seldom decides matters of importance. Decisions on policy matters pass it by. There is little it can do to unify the party. The national committee is, in sum, anything but a powerful force in the politics of each party.

Factors Contributing to Decentralization   It is no happenstance that the national parties lead a furtive existence, under ordinary circumstances visible only during presidential election campaigns. The situation could hardly be otherwise, given the legal and constitutional characteristics of the American political system. In the first place, as we noted in the previous chapter, a decentralized party system appears to be the natural concomitant of a decentralized governmental system. American parties must find their place within a federal system where powers and responsibilities lie with fifty states as well

---

[1] History dictates the same course. Disturbed by congressional opposition to certain New Deal legislation, President Franklin D. Roosevelt attempted in 1938 to "purge" several southern Democrats by openly endorsing their primary opponents. His action ended in embarrassment for him and disaster for his plan, for the voters' response was to elect the very men he had marked for defeat. The lesson is evident that national party leaders must tread warily on local party grounds.

[2] One exception can be noted. During the 89th Congress (1965–1966), the House Democratic caucus, in an unusual exercise of disciplinary powers, took away the seniority rights of two southern Democrats who had publicly endorsed the Republican presidential candidate, Barry Goldwater, in the 1964 election. Nothing would have happened to them had their apostasy been confined to opposing their party in Congress.

as with the national government. The basic laws that both regulate and promote party activity are the products of state legislatures rather than of Congress. Of particular importance, responsibility for the design of the electoral system in which the parties compete is given to the states, not to the nation. Not surprisingly, party organizations have been molded by the electoral laws under which they contest for power. A vast number of local and state power centers have developed around the thousands of governmental units and elective offices found in the states and localities. With his distinctive constituency (frequently a "safe" district), his own coterie of supporters, and, often, his own channels to campaign money, the typical officeholder has a remarkable amount of freedom in defining his relations to party groups. The organization's well-being and his well-being are not necessarily identical. To press this point, it is not too much to say that officeholders are steadily engaged in the process of evaluating party claims and objectives in the light of their own career aspirations. When the party's claims and the officeholder's aspirations fail to converge, the party ordinarily loses out. To cut short a long story, our decentralized governmental system is the principal sponsor of legal-constitutional arrangements that, on the one hand, often immobilize national party agencies and, on the other hand, open up an extraordinary range of political choices to subnational parties and to individual party candidates.

For all of its significance for the party system and the distinctiveness of American politics, however, federalism is but one of several explanations for the decentralization of the major parties. Another constitutional provision, separation of powers, also contributes to the dispersal of governmental and party power. One of the frequent by-products of this system is the emergence of a truncated party majority—that is, a condition under which one party controls one or both houses of the legislature and the other party controls the executive. At worst this leads to a dreary succession of narrow partisan clashes between the branches; at best it may contribute occasionally to the clarification of certain differences between the parties; at no time does it contribute a particle to the development and maintenance of party responsibility for a program of public policy. A glance at Table 4 will reveal the dimensions of this "party problem" in the American states. Over the period 1952–1966, for example, nearly one-half of all gubernatorial-legislative elections led to divided party control of the branches. The pattern at the national level has been much the same.

A third factor contributing to the decentralization of American parties is the method used to make nominations. It was noted earlier that nominations for national office are sorted out and settled at the local level, ordinarily without interference of any sort by national party functionaries. One of the principal supports of local control over this activity is the direct primary. Its use virtually guarantees that candidates for national office will be tailored to

Table 4

Elections in 32 States, 1930–1950, and in 37 States,
1952–1966, Showing Relation of Governor to
Legislature in Terms of Party Control*

Relation Between Governor and Legislature	1930–1950 (32 STATES)		1952–1966 (37 STATES)	
	Number	Percent	Number	Percent
Governor Opposed	126	35.7	133	46.8
Governor Unopposed	227	64.3	151	53.2
	353	100.0	284	100.0

* For the period 1930–1950, fourteen states are excluded because one party continuously held the governorship and both houses of the legislature. These one-party states, mainly Democratic, were Alabama, Arkansas, Florida, Georgia, Louisiana, Mississippi, New Hampshire, North Carolina, Oklahoma, South Carolina, Tennessee, Texas, Vermont, and Virginia. During the period 1952–1966, New Hampshire, Oklahoma, and Vermont entered the ranks of "competitive" states. Minnesota and Nebraska are excluded because they have nonpartisan legislatures. Alaska's tabulations begin with 1958 and Hawaii's with 1959.

Source: The 1930–1950 data are drawn from V. O. Key, Jr., and Corrine Silverman, "Party and Separation of Powers: A Panorama of Practice in the States," in Carl J. Friedrich and J. Kenneth Galbraith (eds.), *Public Policy* (Cambridge, Mass.: Harvard University, Graduate School of Public Administration, 1954), Table 3, p. 389. The 1952–1966 data appear in William J. Keefe and Morris S. Ogul, *The American Legislative Process: Congress and the States* (Englewood Cliffs, N.J.: Prentice-Hall, 1968), p. 118.

the measure of local specifications. Consider this analysis by Austin Ranney and Willmoore Kendall:

> A party's *national* leaders can affect the kind of representatives and senators who come to Washington bearing the party's label only by enlisting the support of the state and local party organizations concerned; and they cannot be sure of doing so even then. Assume, for example, that the local leaders have decided to support the national leaders in an attempt to block the renomination of a maverick congressman, and are doing all they can. There is still nothing to prevent the rank and file, who may admire the incumbent's "independence," from ignoring the leaders' wishes and renominating him. The direct primary, in other words, is *par excellence* a system for maintaining *local* control of nominations; and as long as American localities continue to be so different from one another in economic interests, culture, and political attitudes, the national parties are likely to retain their present ideological heterogeneity and their tendency to show differing degrees of cohesion from issue to issue.[3]

A fourth important explanation for the decentralization of American parties can be found in the financing of political campaigns. Few, if any,

[3] Austin Ranney and Willmoore Kendall, *Democracy and the American Party System* (New York: Harcourt Brace Jovanovich, 1956), p. 497. Another comprehensive analysis of the decentralization of American parties may be found in David B. Truman's essay on "Federalism and the Party System" in Arthur W. MacMahon (ed.), *Federalism: Mature and Emergent* (New York: Doubleday, 1955), pp. 115–136.

campaign resources are more important than money. A large proportion of the political money donated in any year is given directly to the campaign organizations of individual candidates rather than to the party organizations. Moreover, many candidates are sufficiently wealthy to be able to finance all or a large part of their own campaigns. It goes without saying that a candidate who can "bankroll" himself is automatically in a strong position vis-à-vis the party organization. His money virtually guarantees his independence.

Finally, there is a pervasive spirit of localism that dominates American politics and contributes to the deconcentration of political power. There are literally countless ways in which local interests find expression in national politics. Even the presidential nominating convention may become an arena for the settlement of local and state political struggles. Conflicts within state delegations are frequently resolved by the faction that succeeds in identifying and supporting the winning presidential nominee. The cost of backing the "wrong" candidate may be exceedingly high for the losing faction. Very likely some careers will be jeopardized and perhaps cut short; almost certainly members of the losing faction will find both their access to the nominee and their prospects for patronage severely diminished. For a very good reason, national conventions will always have a strong infusion of local politics. The men and women who compose it are, first and foremost, state and local political leaders. They come to the convention not only to select a presidential nominee but also to put new life into their own careers and to advance the interests of their localities.

Congress has always shown a remarkable hospitality to the idea that governmental power should be decentralized. A great deal of the major legislation that has been passed in recent decades, for example, has been designed in such a way as to make state and local governments participants in the development and implementation of public policies.[4] Locally based political organizations have been strengthened as a result. A basic explanation for Congress's defense of state and local governments lies in the backgrounds of the congressmen themselves. Above all else, congressmen are local products. Unlike most business and political executives, most congressmen reside all their lives in their original hometowns. A substantial majority of them will have been elected to state or local office prior to their election to Congress. (See Table 5, which points up the sharply different career patterns of congressional leaders and administration leaders.) They are steeped in local lore, think in local terms, meet frequently with local representatives, and work for local advantage. Their steady attention to the local dimensions of national policy helps to energize local political organization.

---

[4] See Morton Grodzins, "American Political Parties and the American System," *Western Political Quarterly*, XIII (December 1960), pp. 974–998.

Table 5
Experience of National Political Leaders in State
and Local Government*

OFFICES HELD	CONGRESSIONAL LEADERS		ADMINISTRATION LEADERS	
	1903	*1963*	*1903*	*1963*
Any state or local office	75%	64%	49%	17%
Elective local office	55	46	22	5
State legislature	47	30	17	3
Appointive state office	12	10	20	7
Governor	16	9	5	4

* Source: Samuel P. Huntington, "Congressional Responses to the Twentieth Century," in David B. Truman, ed., *The Congress and America's Future* (Englewood Cliffs, N.J.: Prentice-Hall, 1965), p. 14.

The Power of Officeholders   The structure, tone, and mood of American parties bear the heavy imprint of decentralization. This concept, more than any other, brings into focus the essential weakness of national party leaders and institutions. But to stress this characteristic is perhaps to create an illusion of great organizational strength among state and local party units. In point of fact, however, only a few state and local party organizations, *qua* organizations, have any real strength. James M. Burns makes the point this way:

> At no level, except in a handful of industrial states, do state parties have the attributes of organization. They lack extensive dues-paying memberships; hence they number many captains and sergeants but few foot soldiers. They do a poor job of raising money for themselves as organizations, or even for their candidates. They lack strong and imaginative leadership of their own. They cannot control their most vital function—the nomination of their candidates. Except in a few states, such as Ohio, Connecticut, and Michigan, our parties are essentially collections of small cliques and they are often shunted aside by the politicians who understand political power. Most of the state parties are at best mere jousting grounds for embattled politicians; at worst they simply do not exist, as in the case of Republicans in the rural South or Democrats in the rural Midwest.[5]

The malaise that tends to characterize party organizations at all levels of government results in a concentration of power in the hands of public officeholders and candidates for public office. Sometimes in their own names and sometimes in the name of their party, they assume the critical functions associated with campaigns and elections. In most jurisdictions it is the officeholders (or aspirants) who develop issues and strategies, who recruit the

[5] James M. Burns, *The Deadlock of Democracy: Four Party Politics in America* (Englewood Cliffs, N.J.: Prentice-Hall, 1963), pp. 236–237.

corps of campaign workers, who raise the necessary political money, who mobilize the voters, and who carry the party banner. Their power comes not as the result of wresting leadership from party officials but rather from taking over campaign responsibilities that otherwise would be met inadequately, or perhaps not at all, by the formal party organization.[6]

Party Competition Varies Sharply from State to State and from Office to Office

Familiar and conventional interpretations in American politics are never easy to abandon. Old labels persist even though their descriptive power has been sharply eroded; such is the case in the designation of the American two-party system. Vigorous two-party competition in all jurisdictions is, of course, clearly unattainable. No one should expect it. What surprises, however, is how little two-party competition is to be found in certain electoral districts of the nation. The American party system is in places and at times strongly two-party, and in other places and at other times, dominantly one-party. In addition, there are states and localities in which factional politics within one or both of the major parties is so pervasive and persistent as to suggest the presence of a multiple-party system. Competition between the parties is a condition not to be taken for granted, despite the popular tendency to bestow the two-party label upon American politics.

Competitiveness in Presidential and Congressional Elections Although in many states and localities there is little more than a veneer of competitiveness between the parties, this is not the case in presidential elections. Contests for this office provide the best single example of authentic two-party competition, particularly in recent decades. With but one exception in all two-party presidential contests since 1940, the losing presidential candidate has received at least 45 percent of the popular vote; the lone exception occurred in 1964 when Barry Goldwater received slightly under 39 percent of the vote. Several recent elections have been extraordinarily close: in 1960 John Kennedy received 49.7 percent of the popular vote to Richard Nixon's 49.5 percent; in a turnabout in 1968 Nixon obtained 43.4 percent to Hubert Humphrey's 42.7 percent (with George Wallace receiving 13.5 percent). The plain fact is that the two major parties are now so evenly matched in presidential contests that the losing party has excellent reason to expect that it can win the office within an election or two.

A view of presidential elections from the states is worth examining. In the

---

[6] See Burns, *The Deadlock of Democracy*, pp. 239–240.

last two decades there has been a sharp decline in the number of one-party states and regions in presidential elections. The point is readily verified in Figure 1, which shows the tempo of Republican growth in the once solid Democratic South. The watershed in southern political history appears to have been 1952. Dwight D. Eisenhower carried four southern states (Florida, Tennessee, Texas, and Virginia), narrowly missing victories in several other states, while receiving over 48 percent of the popular vote throughout the South. Almost as remarkable was Richard Nixon's victory in 1968. In the District of Columbia and thirty-nine states outside the South, Hubert H. Humphrey led Nixon by about 30,000 votes; in the eleven southern states Nixon led Humphrey by over 500,000 votes. A similar, if less spectacular, decline in one-party domination shows up in certain traditionally Republican strongholds. At one time immoderately Republican, such states as Maine, New Hampshire, and Vermont are no longer "in the bag." Each presidential election puts a further strain on old party loyalties. It is a good guess that future presidential elections will continue to be closely competitive, often decided by thin margins in a handful of states.

Congressional elections are another story. Indeed, the principal attribute that most congressional districts have in common is a history of one-party domination. One-party domination in congressional elections is not confined, as the popular stereotype would have it, to the Democratic South or the Republican Midwest; quite the contrary, it is the dominant pattern in all sections of the country. Table 6 shows the extent to which House and Senate elections have been diverted from the main stream of competitive politics at the national level. In most recent elections about 15 to 20 percent of the House elections have been in the "marginal" (or competitive) category—

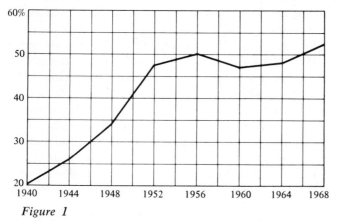

Figure 1

Republican Percentage of Two-Party Presidential
Vote, 1940–1968, Eleven Southern States

Table 6
Marginal, Safer, and Uncontested Seats in Elections
to U.S. House of Representatives and Senate,
1962–1970, by Percentage of Total Seats*

Election Margin	HOUSE					SENATE				
	1962	1964	1966	1968	1970	1962	1964	1966	1968	1970
Seats won by Democrats, by less than 55% of the vote (Marginal)	10.4%	14.2%	7.6%	10.6%	6.0%	33.3%	26.5%	20.6%	21.2%	21.2%
Seats won by Republicans, by less than 55% of the vote (Marginal)	8.0	11.3	9.4	6.0	6.5	15.4	17.7	8.8	27.3	21.2
Seats won by Democrats, by 55% or more of the vote (Safer)	38.9	44.9	39.3	37.0	42.1	28.2	50.0	20.6	30.3	45.5
Seats won by Republicans, by 55% or more of the vote (Safer)	31.9	20.6	32.9	36.3	34.2	20.5	2.9	41.2	15.1	12.0
Uncontested seats	10.8	9.0	10.8	10.1	11.2	2.6	2.9	8.8	6.1	0.0
Total	100.0	100.0	100.0	100.0	100.0	100.0	100.0	100.0	100.0	100.0

* Source: William J. Keefe and Morris S. Ogul, *The American Legislative Process: Congress and the States* (Englewood Cliffs, N.J.: Prentice-Hall, 1968), p. 110; *1969 Congressional Quarterly Almanac*, pp. 1202–1238; and *Congressional Quarterly Weekly Report* (November 6, 1970), pp. 2771–2778.

that is, elections in which the winning candidate receives less than 55 percent of the vote. In only about 70 to 100 districts out of 435 is there ordinarily any chance that the incumbent party will lose—so safe are the vast majority of congressional districts. Though somewhat more competitive than those of the House, Senate elections nevertheless usually result in control by the same party.

Table 7 helps to fill out this account of noncompetitiveness at the congressional level. In most election years at least 90 percent of the incumbents in the House and Senate are reelected. Ordinarily, not many incumbents fall by the wayside in the primaries. All this comes down to the fact that Congress is an arena for two-party politics not because its members are produced by competitive environments but because *both* parties have managed to develop and to maintain large blocs of "noncompetitive" seats. American politics, it seems, has been fashioned out of such anomalies.

Competitiveness at the State Level   A glance at Table 8, borrowed from a study by Austin Ranney, reveals the wide range of competitiveness in the fifty states. The degree of interparty competition was calculated for each state

Table 7
Number and Percentage of Incumbents Who
Won Reelection, 1956–1968.*

Year	Incumbents Seeking Re-election	Lost Primary		Lost General Election		Reelected	
		HOUSE OF REPRESENTATIVES					
1956	411	6	1.5%	16	3.9%	389	94.6%
1958	394	3	0.8	37	9.4	354	89.8
1960	403	5	1.2	26	6.5	372	92.3
1962	393	11	2.8	14	3.6	368	93.6
1964	397	8	2.0	44	11.1	345	86.9
1966	407	5	1.2	40	9.8	362	89.0
1968	409	4	1.0	9	2.2	396	96.8
		SENATE**					
1956	30	0		4	13.3	26	86.7
1958	26	0		9	34.6	17	65.4
1960	28	0		1	3.6	27	96.4
1962	30	0		3	10.0	27	90.0
1964	30	0		2	6.7	28	93.3
1966	31	2	6.5	1	3.2	28	90.3
1968	28	4	14.3	4	14.3	20	71.4

* Source: From *Congress and the Public Trust*, by James C. Kirby, Jr., Copyright © 1970 by The Association of the Bar of the City of New York Fund, Inc. Reprinted by permission of Atheneum Publishers.

** The term "incumbent" excludes those appointed to fill out unexpired terms. During this period only four such appointees served longer than one year. All four were governors who resigned to accept appointment to the Senate, and all were subsequently defeated.

Table 8
The Fifty States Classified According to
Degree of Interparty Competition*

One-Party Democratic	Modified One-Party Democratic	Two-Party		Modified One-Party Republican
South Carolina (1.0000)	Virginia (.8795)	Alaska (.6767)	Pennsylvania (.4050)	Wisconsin (.2997)
Georgia (.9915)	North Carolina (.8793)	Missouri (.6603)	California (.3930)	New Hampshire (.2680)
Louisiana (.9867)	Tennessee (.8715)	Rhode Island (.6327)	Nebraska (.3875)	Iowa (.2495)
Mississippi (.9805)	Oklahoma (.8193)	Washington (.5647)	Illinois (.3847)	Kansas (.2415)
Texas (.9590)	Kentucky (.7650)	Delaware (.5420)	Idaho (.3780)	Maine (.2405)
Alabama (.9565)	Arizona (.7490)	Nevada (.5263)	Michigan (.3770)	South Dakota (.2320)
Arkansas (.9427)	West Virginia (.7223)	Massachusetts (.5227)	New Jersey (.3605)	North Dakota (.1860)
Florida (.9220)	Maryland (.7137)	Hawaii (.4897)	Indiana (.3545)	Vermont (.1760)
	New Mexico (.7023)	Colorado (.4827)	Oregon (.3545)	
		Montana (.4695)	Ohio (.3523)	
		Minnesota (.4610)	Wyoming (.3470)	
		Utah (.4605)	New York (.3173)	
		Connecticut (.4420)		

* Source: Austin Ranney, "Parties in State Politics," in Herbert Jacob and Kenneth Vines (eds.), *Politics in the American States*, p. 65. Copyright © 1965, Little, Brown and Company, Inc. Reprinted by permission.

by blending four separate state "scores": the average percentage of the popular vote received by Democratic gubernatorial candidates, the average percentage of Democratic seats in the state senate, the average percentage of Democratic seats in the state house of representatives, and the percentage of all terms for governor, senate, and house in which the Democrats were in control. Taken together, these percentages produced an "index of competitiveness," ranging (theoretically) from .0000 (total Republican domination) to 1.0000 (total Democratic domination). At midpoint, .5000, perfect competition would exist between the parties.[7]

[7] Austin Ranney, "Parties in State Politics," in Herbert Jacob and Kenneth Vines (eds.), *Politics in the American States*, pp. 64–65. Copyright © 1965, Little, Brown and Company, Inc.

In one-half of the American states party competition for *state* offices lacks an authentic ring. Over the period of this study, 1946 to 1963, eight states (all southern) were classified as one-party Democratic; another seventeen states were designated as either modified one-party Democratic or modified one-party Republican. Twenty-five states met the test of two-party competition.

Two particularly interesting correlations with competitiveness appear. One concerns the relationship between one-party domination and membership in the Confederacy—all eight one-party Democratic states withdrew from the Union, as did North Carolina, Tennessee, and Virginia (all modified one-party Democratic states). It is plain that for many of the states that today have a low level of party competition (in particular for state offices), the Civil War was the great divide. The second correlation to be noted centers on urbanization: not surprisingly, the two-party states are significantly more urbanized than the other states. In similar fashion these states are also distinguished by having high per capita incomes, a significant proportion of "foreign stock," a high proportion of labor devoted to manufacturing, and a low proportion of labor devoted to agriculture.[8]

The degree of interparty competitiveness cannot, of course, be measured only in terms of the struggle for state offices, as this study notes. Some of the states in the one-party or modified one-party categories during this period had vigorous two-party competition in certain presidential, congressional, and senatorial elections. Virginia, for example, classified as a modified one-party Democratic state, has long had a large number of "presidential Republican" voters. Indeed, this nominally Democratic state voted Republican in four of the six presidential elections between 1948 and 1968. Competitiveness must therefore be explored along several dimensions.

Competitiveness at the Office Level Party competition varies sharply not only between states but between *offices* in the same state. Figure 2, the work of Joseph Schlesinger, reveals the complexity inherent in the concept of competitiveness. To unravel the figure, examine the location of each state office on the horizontal and vertical axes. The horizontal axis shows the extent to which the parties have controlled each office over the period of the study; the vertical axis shows the rate of turnover in control of the office between the parties. It is readily apparent that some offices are steadfastly held by one party (for example, governor, Wisconsin; comptroller, Maryland) and that other offices are genuinely competitive (for example, senator, Maryland; lieutenant governor, Ohio). Wide variations exist within each state. Taking the northern states as a group, there is less competition for seats in Congress

[8] Ranney, "Parties in State Politics," pp. 67–69.

than for any other office. By contrast, the offices of governor and senator are the most competitive—even these offices, however, are not significantly competitive.

Overall, the pattern of competition depicted in Figure 2 testifies to the inability of state parties to compete for and to control a range of offices. To emphasize a point made earlier, the figure suggests, albeit subtly, that the

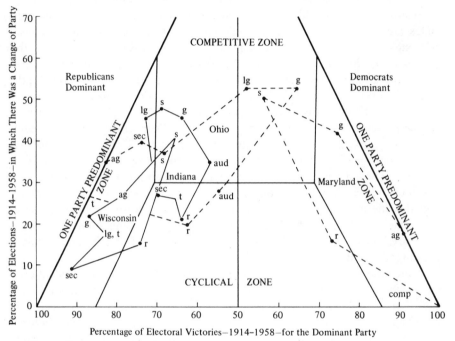

Figure 2
Party Competition for Individual Offices
(Selected States)

Office Key

g:	Governor
s:	Senator
r:	Congressman
lg:	Lieutenant governor
sec:	Secretary of State
ag:	Attorney General
aud:	Auditor
t:	Treasurer
comp:	Comptroller

". . . the more centrally located on the horizontal axis the more competitive an office was in overall terms; the higher on the diagram the more rapid the rate of turnover; and correspondingly, the lower on the diagram an office falls, the longer the cycles of one-party control, regardless of the degree of overall competition."

Source: Joseph A. Schlesinger, "The Structure of Competition for Office in the American States," *Behavioral Science*, V (July 1960), p. 203.

successful officeholder is one who develops and maintains his own campaign resources, knowing that the party organization is about as likely to be a spectator to his career as a guardian of it.

Competitiveness in a One-Party Environment No discussion of American one-party systems can proceed far without encountering the peculiar and inevitable dynamic of such systems: factional politics. Not by any means are all one-party systems alike in their factional characteristics. Some one-party states are characterized by multifactionalism, and others, by bifactionalism. Although it is true, of course, that factional struggles sometimes occur within parties in a two-party system, their significance is ordinarily much less pronounced than in heavily one-party jurisdictions, especially those of the South.[9]

Factionalism in the South grew up around the Democratic primary. Because of the weakness of the Republican party, the "real" election in most southern states usually has taken place in the Democratic primary. Candidates winning at this stage ordinarily have run little risk of defeat in the general election, perhaps not even having a Republican opponent with whom to contend. The absence of strong interparty competition (especially for state and local offices) has inflated the importance of the dominant party's primary, and this in turn has led to a freewheeling, individualistic politics in which candidates of all kinds struggle for the Democratic nomination in a virtual "no-party" environment.[10] This pattern is changing, of course, as a result of growing Republican strength in the South.

Some southern states have been characterized by a persistent bifactionalism, with two relatively well-organized groups contesting election after election. For several decades following the arrival of Huey Long on the scene, the principal political division in Louisiana (Democratic) politics was between the Long and the anti-Long factions, the first identified with the low income groups (both in rural areas and New Orleans), and the second, with the conservative elements of business and agriculture.[11] The Louisiana experience shows that in limited measure bifactional struggles resemble two-party

[9] The leading studies of southern factionalism are V. O. Key, Jr., *Southern Politics in State and Nation* (New York: Knopf, 1949) and Allan P. Sindler, *Huey Long's Louisiana* (Baltimore: Johns Hopkins Press, 1956).

[10] The presence of numerous candidates in southern Democratic primaries often has meant that the vote is highly fragmented, with no candidate receiving a majority. To inject the majority idea into the election system, southern states employ a "runoff" primary. If no candidate garners a majority of the vote in the first primary, a second or runoff primary is held several weeks later between the two candidates who received the most votes. With the field thus narrowed to two, one of the candidates is assured of a majority.

[11] Currently, Louisiana would be classified as a multifactional state. See Donald R. Matthews and James W. Prothro, *Negroes and the New Southern Politics* (New York: Harcourt Brace Jovanovich, 1966), pp. 159–160.

competition; there were recognized sets of leaders, identifiable policy orientations, well-developed campaign organizations, and more or less stable popular
followings. More typical is multifactionalism, which is characterized by
numerous candidates for the same office, each with his own personal organization (ordinarily strong in his own and neighboring counties and weak
statewide), each concerned with his own survival. Candidacies are rarely linked
together by any form of "ticket," as has been used in Louisiana. Where multifactionalism prevails, it is virtually impossible for the voter to sort through the
tes, identifying those with something of a common ideology, in order
a group of men who are disposed to cooperate with one another.
multifactionalism produces a free-for-all; candidates of all stripes vie
e another in a barrage of charges and counter-charges, leaving the
te confused as to the direction the government will take once the new
ve come to power.
onal politics lack structure and coherence, even in a bifactional state.
the superficial resemblance of bifactional politics to two-party politics,
es that separate the factions are never as clear-cut as they are in a two-
ystem. Uncertainty plagues political careers. Aspiring politicians link
ndidacies to one or the other of the two factions, but their affiliations
ft from one election to the next. The paths of advancement are never
marked, either for potential candidates or for officeholders. Improbable
s develop, only to disappear as frustrations mount and as new oppor-
come into view. By and large, the faction that wins is unprepared to
generalized control over the government. Overall, the label of the
n power conceals more than it illuminates. And there is slim prospect
e voter will be able to make sharp distinctions among the candidates
or, following the election, hold any group even roughly accountable for its
performance in office.

The Persistent Two-Party System in America Despite the existence of one-
party systems here and there, political competition in the United States usually
comes down to competition between the two major parties, Democratic and
Republican. It is not easy to depict clearly why American politics has been
hospitable to a two-party rather than a multiple-party system, as in many
European democracies. Without attempting a detailed analysis of this complex
question, we can summarize the principal hypotheses that have been offered.
Less than "laws" and more than hunches, they include the following explanations.

A familiar explanation is that election of members of the U.S. House of
Representatives from single-member districts by plurality vote helps to support
the two-party pattern. Under this arrangement a single candidate is elected in
each district, and he needs to receive only a plurality of the vote. There is

slight inducement for third-party candidates to run, since the prospects are poor that they could defeat the candidates of the two major parties. On the other hand, if congressmen were elected under a proportional representation scheme, with several members chosen in each district, third-party candidates would undoubtedly have a better chance of winning some seats. Third parties are up against the same obstacle in presidential elections: only one party can capture the presidency. For this office the nation as a whole takes on the cast of a single-member district. Each state's electoral votes are awarded as a unit to the candidate receiving a plurality of the popular vote; all other popular votes are in effect wasted. In 1968, for example, George Wallace, candidate of the American Independent party, received about five million popular votes in states *outside* the South but won electoral votes only in the five southern states he carried. If electoral votes were divided in proportion to popular votes in each state, third-party candidates would likely make a bigger dent in the electoral vote totals of the major parties. Electoral practices in the United States, it is plain, are hard on third parties.

The diversity and flexibility that characterizes the two major parties also contribute to the preservation of the two-party system. The policy orientations of the parties are rarely so firmly fixed as to preclude a shift in emphasis or direction in order to attract emerging interests within the electorate. Moreover, each party is made up of officeholders with different views; almost any political group, as a result, can discover some officials who share its values and predilections and who are willing to represent its point of view. The adaptability of the parties and officeholders not only permits them to siphon off support that otherwise might contribute to the development of third parties but also creates a great deal of slack in the political system. Groups pressing for change know that there is always some prospect that they can win acceptance for their positions within the existing party framework.

Another central explanation for the durability of the two-party system in America is found in a tradition of dualism. Early political struggles took place between those who favored adoption of the Constitution and those who opposed it. Subsequently dualism was reflected in struggles between Federalists and Anti-Federalists and, later still, between Democrats and Whigs. Since the Civil War the main party battle has been fought out between Democrats and Republicans. In sum, the main elements of conflict within the American political system have ordinarily found expression in competition between two dominant groups of politicians and their followings. This, in a nutshell, is the essence of American party history. Third parties have cropped up from time to time to challenge the major parties, but their lives ordinarily have been short and uneventful—so deep-seated is the attachment of most Americans to inherited institutions and practices.[12]

[12] For analysis of the dualism theme, see V. O. Key, Jr., *Politics, Parties, & Pressure Groups*, pp. 207–208.

A profusion of other themes might be explored in seeking to account for the two-party character of American politics. Election law, for example, makes it difficult for all but the most well-organized and well-financed third parties to gain a place on the ballot; in presidential elections they must struggle in state after state to recruit campaign workers and funds and to collect signatures for their nominating petitions. Even audiences may be hard to come by. Moreover, because the risk of failure looms so large, new political organizations must strain to find acceptable candidates to run under their banner; aspiring politicians are not notable for their willingness to take quixotic risks for the sake of ideology or principle, particularly if there is some chance that a career in one of the major parties is available. The extraordinary costs of organizing and conducting major campaigns, the difficulties that attend the search for men and women to man party outposts, and the frustrations that plague efforts to cut the cords that bind American voters to the traditional parties all serve to inhibit the formation and maintenance of third parties. Finally, it appears that the restless impulse for new alternatives that often dominates other nations, leading to the formation of new parties, is found less commonly in the United States. Not all American citizens, of course, are wholly satisfied with the political, economic, and social systems of the country. Recent years have witnessed a storm of protests against "establishment politics" by certain college and university students. Nonetheless, there are few indications that the public as a whole is in the mood for a sharp change in the nation's basic political institutions.

Parties as Coalitions

Viewed from afar, the American major party is likely to appear as a miscellaneous collection of individual activists and voters, banded together in some fashion in order to attempt to gain control of government. But there is more shadow than substance in that view, for when the party is brought into sharp focus, its basic coalitional character is revealed. The point is simple but important: the party is much less a collection of individuals than it is a collection of social interests and groups. In the words of Maurice Duverger, "A party is not a community but a collection of communities, a union of small groups dispersed throughout the country. . . ."[13]

Functioning within a vastly heterogeneous society, the major parties have naturally assumed a coalitional form. Groups of all kinds—social, economic, religious, and ethnic—are organized to press demands on the political order. In the course of defending or advancing their interests, they contribute substantial energy to the political process—through generating innovations,

[13] Maurice Duverger, *Political Parties* (New York: Wiley, 1965), p. 17.

posing alternative policies, recruiting and endorsing candidates, conducting campaigns, and so on. It is safe to say that no party seriously contesting for office could ignore the constellation of groups in American political life.

Party leaders are accustomed to thinking in coalition terms. The candidates to be slated, the issues to be developed, the decisions on the allocation of resources, and the jobs to be filled—all such choices are made with one eye on the coalitions that compose the party and the other eye on the overall objectives of the party. The test of party leadership, perhaps especially at the local level, is its capacity to "harmonize" group interests, bringing them into accord with each other and with the broad goals of the party. The picture portrayed in these interviews with Detroit party leaders, taken from a recent study by Samuel Eldersveld, suggests the central tasks posed for party management:

> The district chairman has to be a Sherlock Holmes in the Republican party. We have, as you know, many splits in our party, and there is a constant battle of wits as to who is for whom. You have to be flexible—to meet these people on their own level, talk shop, pat them on the back, and get the work out of them.

> In our district we have a Polish section, a Negro section, a Jewish section, and any number of smaller groups. I have to be a jack of all trades. My job is to get as many people in these groups happy as I can and see that they get the votes out.[14]

Although the coalitions that make up the parties may look illogical and untidy to the outsider, they are fundamental to party organization and strategy. The capacity of a party to win an election depends on the skill of its leaders in putting together or maintaining a majority coalition of groups, some of which will hold sharply conflicting views. The presence of incompatible groups within the same party coalition is not uncommon. Since the early days of the New Deal, for example, the Democratic coalition has been the principal home of southern Democrats, northern Negroes, and a variety of ethnic groups (Polish, Italian, and so on) located mainly in large northern cities; conflicts between these groups have been inevitable as civil rights questions have gained in significance and visibility. The urban working classes, Catholics, and Jews have also been important elements in the Democratic coalition. In counterpoise, the Republican coalition in recent decades has drawn a disproportionate number of supporters from such groups as big business, industry, farmers, small-town and rural dwellers, small businessmen, Protestants, suburbanites, and "old stock" Americans. It, too, is an uneasy alliance.

The generalization that describes the American major parties as coalitions

---

[14] Samuel J. Eldersveld, *Political Parties: A Behavioral Analysis*, © 1964 by Rand McNally & Company, Chicago, pp. 75–76.

cannot be advanced without a caveat or two. No group, it should be emphasized, is exclusively identified with one party; a significant number of union members, for example, will always be found voting Republican even though their unions endorse and support candidates of the Democratic party. Moreover, coalitions are always in flux as members grow restive over developments within their party and attentive to the attractions of the other party. In recent years, for example, southern Democrats have found it painful to remain within the coalition that makes up the national Democratic party. Disillusioned over the liberal thrust of the party, many life-long southern Democrats bolted in 1964 to support Barry Goldwater. In even greater number they moved into the ranks of the American Independent party in 1968, voting for George Wallace in preference to Hubert Humphrey or Richard Nixon. American parties are fragile because they are coalitions, held together by the baling wire of generality and promise. What is surprising is that they hold together in campaigns as well as they do.

The American major party is anything but clannish. It will devote a friendly ear to almost any request. All groups are invited to support it, and in some measure, all do. Ordinarily, everything about the major party, functioning at the election stage, represents a triumph for those who press for accommodation in American politics. Platforms and candidate speeches, offering something to almost everyone, provide the hard evidence that the parties attempt to be inclusive rather than exclusive in their appeals and to draw in a wide rather than a narrow band of voters. "No matter how devoted a party leadership may be to its bedrock elements," V. O. Key observed, "it attempts to picture itself as a gifted synthesizer of concord among the elements of society. A party must act as if it were all the people rather than some of them; it must fiercely deny that it speaks for a single interest."[15]

But problems develop once the election is over and the party has been placed in office. It is at this point that the coalition put together so carefully in the campaign runs the risk of flying apart. The behavior of the Democratic party in Congress offers a good example of the coalition dilemma. Table 9 reports on the extent to which southern Democrats have split off from northern Democrats at the roll-call stage in a number of recent sessions. The table is a study in divergence: on roughly one-fifth to one-third of all roll calls a majority of southern Democrats opposed a majority of "northern" (all other) Democrats.

The evidence of Table 9 is that a great deal of disagreement hides behind the party label, especially in the case of the congressional Democrats. When party coalitions come apart in Congress, biparty coalitions are often brought to life. The most persistent and successful biparty coalition in the history of Congress has been the "conservative coalition," formed by a majority of south-

[15] V. O. Key, Jr., *Politics, Parties, & Pressure Groups*, p. 221.

Table 9
Northern vs. Southern Democrats in Congress*

Year	Total Roll Call Votes Both Chambers	North-South Democratic Splits**	Percentage of Splits
1957	207	64	31%
1958	293	84	29
1959	302	83	27
1960	300	119	40
1961	320	107	33
1962	348	74	21
1963	348	84	24
1964	308	75	24
1965	459	160	35
1966	428	124	29
1967	560	148	26
1968	514	173	34
1969	422	153	36
1970	684	233	34

* This table is used with the permission of the Congressional Quarterly Service. See the *Congressional Quarterly Weekly Report*, January 29, 1971, p. 254.
** A majority of voting southern Democrats opposed to a majority of voting northern Democrats.

ern Democrats and a majority of Republicans. In existence in one form or another since the late 1930s, this coalition comes together on essentially the same policy issues that divide northern from southern Democrats. It is no exaggeration to say that the most effective majority in some recent sessions of Congress has been the southern Democrat-Republican coalition. Indeed, about the only recent Congress in which a lid was put on the coalition's power was the 89th Congress (1965–1966)—a brief interval in which the Democratic majority, under President Lyndon Johnson, was so overpowering that even the defection of many southerners ordinarily could not bring the party down.

Parties of Ideological Heterogeneity

To win elections and gain power is the unabashedly practical aim of the major party. As suggested previously, this calls for a strategy of coalition-building in which the policy goals of the groups and candidates brought under the party umbrella are subordinated to their capacity to contribute to party victory. The key to party success is its adaptability, its willingness "to do business" with groups and individuals holding all variety of views on public policy questions. The natural outcome of a campaign strategy designed to attract all groups (and to repel none) is that the party's ideology is rarely

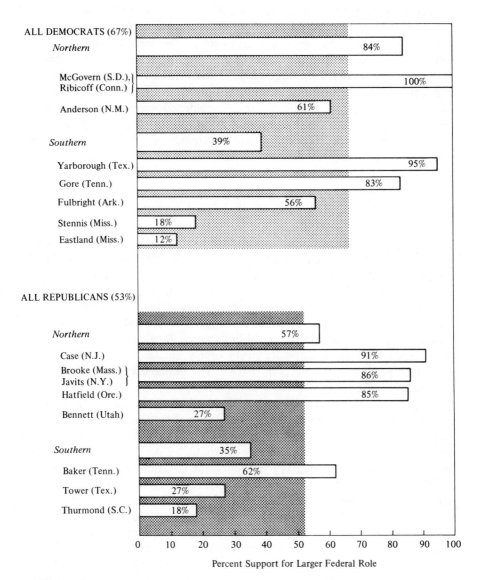

Figure 3

Democratic and Republican Support for Larger
Federal Role, by Section and Individual Members,
90th Congress, U.S. Senate

This graph is adapted from data presented by the *Congressional Quarterly Weekly Report*,
XXVI, November 15, 1968, p. 3130. The states of the Confederacy are classified as "southern,"
while all others are classified as "northern."

brought into sharp focus. It is, in a sense, up for grabs, to be interpreted as individual party members and officeholders see fit. Figure 3 gives a clue to the ideological distance that separates members of the same party in the U.S. Senate on a series of questions involving the role of the federal government. Those senators voting for a larger federal role in the 90th Congress favored such issues as a civil rights bill relating to open housing, federal support for a school lunch program, public housing, heightened support for the federal poverty program, gun control, and medicaid. Viewed in ideological terms, each party is a mass of tensions and contradictions, with party members marching to a variety of different drums.

The Party as an Interest Group

Although American parties are sometimes criticized for their cool detachment from important social issues, the same cannot be said for their attitude toward a band of issues having high relevance for the party, *qua* party. Certain kinds of issues, or policy questions, which come before legislatures present the party with an opportunity to advance its interests as an organization—in much the same fashion as political interest groups attempt to secure or block legislation that would improve or impair their fortunes. There is, Professor E. E. Schattschneider wrote some years ago, both a "private" and a "public" personality within each party.[16] The public dimension of the party is on display when larger questions of public policy are brought before the legislature; as often happens on these questions party lines fail to hold, factions ease away from the party, and biparty coalitions come to life, empowered for the moment as the majority. The party's public appearance, in the judgment of many critics, leaves much to be desired; the fundamental flaw is that the party nominally in control of government, but rent by factionalism and fragmentation, cannot be held responsible by the public for its decisions. The problem is not that party unity collapses on all issues but that it collapses with sufficient frequency to make it less than a dependable agent for carrying out commitments presumably made to the electorate.

In sharp contrast is the private personality of the party. Though it is an exaggeration to argue that the party is engaged in steady introspection, it is surely true, as Schattschneider has observed, that "the party knows its private mind better than it knows its public mind."[17] It has a sharp sense of where the best opportunities lie for partisan advantage, and an equally keen sense of the perils and pitfalls that can threaten or damage party interests. Numerous

[16] From E. E. Schattschneider, *Party Government*, pp. 133–137.
[17] From *Party Government*, by E. E. Schattschneider. Copyright 1942 by E. E. Schattschneider. Reprinted by permission of Holt, Rinehart and Winston, p. 134.

opportunities are available for transmitting benefits to the party organization and its members. Patronage can be extracted from government at all levels; in some jurisdictions there are literally hundreds and thousands of jobs available for distribution to party stalwarts. At the national level the custom of "senatorial courtesy" guarantees that senators will have the dominant voice in the selection of candidates to fill various positions, such as those of district court judges and U.S. marshals. This custom provides that before nominating a person for a position in a state, the President will consult with the senators of that state (if they belong to the same party as he does) to learn their preference for the position. If he should nominate someone objectionable to the senators of that state, the prospects are strong that the Senate as a whole will reject the nominee, irrespective of his qualifications for the position. On questions of this sort—those which touch the careers and political fortunes of members—party unity is both high and predictable.

Legislators have never won reputations for queuing up behind proposals that might limit maneuvering in the interest of their careers or their party's welfare. With only a few exceptions, for example, they have been opponents of plans to extend the merit system, to take judges "out of politics," and to empower independent boards or commissions to assume responsibility for reapportionment and redistricting. There is a private side to such public questions as these—to extend the merit system is to cut back party patronage, to remove judges from the election process is to cut off a career avenue for legislators with their sights on the court, and to give a nonlegislative commission control over redistricting is to run the risk of a major rearrangement of legislative districts and a resultant loss of offices. What is plain is that legislators and the parties they represent take seriously their role as guardians of the welfare of the organization and the personal interests of its members. As a collectivity, the American party is never more resourceful or more cohesive than when it is monitoring party business. And party business, it is worth noting, is about as likely to intrude on the great public questions as it is on those of narrow or parochial concern. Opportunities to advance the party cause—through debate, legislation, or investigations—are limited only by a failure of imagination.

The Ambiguity of Party Membership

For those people who set great store by neat and orderly arrangements, the American major party is vastly disappointing. There are, of course, numerous examples of the party in disarray. A particularly good one, in the judgment of some students of American politics, involves the concept of party "membership."

Who is a party member in the United States? The answer is far from clear, though a stab at the question can be made by considering the legal aspects of party membership. In closed-primary states there are minimum tests of membership. In these states, roughly three-fourths of the total, the person who registers as a Democrat or as a Republican must in some fashion establish the authenticity of his affiliation. Ordinarily this is no more than a pro forma affirmation by the voter that he regards himself as a Democrat or Republican or that he customarily votes for the candidates of one of the parties. In any case, legal party membership in these states is determined by self-classification at the stage of registration; the significance of establishing membership is that each party's primary is open only to members of that party. By contrast, in open-primary states there is no test of party affiliation; the "act" of gaining membership consists merely of the voter's request for the ballot of the party in whose primary he wishes to participate. In certain

"A registered Democrat, yes. But what *kind* of registered Democrat are you?"

Drawing by Alan Dunn; © 1970 The New Yorker Magazine, Inc.

open-primary states the voter is automatically given the ballots of all the parties, with instructions to mark one and discard the rest.

The simple fact is that, apart from primary voting in closed-primary states, membership in an American major party is of slight moment. In effect, anyone who considers himself a Democrat is a Democrat; anyone who considers himself a Republican is a Republican. A citizen may register one way and vote another or not vote at all. No obligations intrude on the party member. He can be a member without applying for admission, a beneficiary without paying dues or contributing to campaigns, a critic without attending meetings, an interpreter without knowing party vocabulary, an apostate without fearing discipline. To the citizen who takes politics casually, it may be the best of all worlds. The typical American is insensitive to the claims, problems, and doctrine of his party. His principal participation in party life is through the act of voting—sometimes for his party and, of course, sometimes not.

The Indomitable Party?

The party in America is at the center of the political process. Nonetheless, its grip on political power is far from secure. To be sure, the men and women who are recruited for party and public offices, the issues that they bring before the electorate, the campaigns in which they participate, and the government that they help to organize and direct—all are influenced by party. The basic problem remains, however, that the party is unable to control all the routes to political power. In some jurisdictions, nonpartisan election systems have been developed to try to remove parties from politics, and to a degree they have succeeded. Moreover, so thoroughly are some states and localities dominated by one party that party itself has come to have little relevance for the kinds of men and women recruited for office or for the voters in need of cues for casting their votes. Devices such as the direct primary have also cut into the power of the party organization, serving in particular to discourage national party agencies from attempting to influence nominations, including those for national office, and to open up the nominating process to all kinds of candidates. Perhaps most important, the growing influence of the mass media, public relations experts, and campaign management firms has diminished the role of party organizations in political campaigns.[18]

The wonder of American politics is that the party system functions as well as it does. From the perspective of party leaders, the American Constitution is a vast wasteland, scarcely capable of supporting vigorous parties; federalism, the separation of powers, checks and balances, and staggered elections all

---

[18] The impact of the mass media and professional campaign management firms on the electorate and the party system is considered in Chapter 6.

have proved inimical to the organization of strong parties. The burden of the evidence is that national and state constitutions were drafted by men suspicious of the concentration of power in any hands; their designs have served to fracture or immobilize party power.[19] The national parties have few powers, and state and local parties are not vastly better off. The party itself is an uneasy coalition of individuals and groups brought together for limited purposes. Within government, power is about as likely to be lodged in nooks and crannies as it is in central party agencies. Conflict within the parties is sometimes as intense as it is between the parties. As for the individual party member, he has a great many rights but virtually no responsibilities for the well-being of the party.

Public disillusionment over the parties places a further strain on their capacities. Many voters believe that the parties have not posed imaginative solutions for such nagging issues as racial injustice, urban decay, and poverty. Similarly, citizens are concerned over the "old" politics that seems to dominate the parties, manifested in a preoccupation with patronage, perquisites, and the welfare of the organization rather than with public policy. The parties also come in for harsh criticism for their apparent willingness to yield to the blandishments of pressure groups and local interests, while too frequently ignoring broad national interests and problems. For many citizens, it is all too clear, the parties appear as starkly conservative institutions, fearful of innovation and unable to shape intelligent responses to contemporary dilemmas. At no time in the last century have the American major parties occupied such troubled ground as they do today.

Despite their present difficulties, it is by no means clear that the major parties are in the process of withering away, to be replaced by government without parties or government by multiple-party coalitions. But stock-taking is surely in order. Viewed broadly, what seems to be required for party revitalization is the development of a new responsiveness within the parties, one that extends to all the interests that comprise the American polity. The importance of restoring the parties ought to be obvious. It is inconceivable that democracy could exist in the absence of a viable party system.

[19] See Burns, *The Deadlock of Democracy*, especially Chapters 1 and 2.

3
Political Parties and the Electoral Process

It is probable that no nation has ever experimented as fully or as fitfully with mechanisms for making nominations as has the United States. The principal sponsor of this experimentation is the federal system itself. Under it, responsibility for the development of election law lies with the states. Their ingenuity, given free rein, has often been remarkable. A wide variety of caucuses, conventions, and primaries—the three principal methods of making nominations—have been tried out in the states. Those devices that have lasted owe their survival not so much to a widespread agreement on their merits as to the inability of opponents to settle upon alternative arrangements and to the general indifference of the public at large to major institutional change.

Nominating Methods

Caucus   The oldest device for making nominations in the United States is the caucus. In use prior to the adoption of the Constitution, the caucus is an informal meeting of political leaders held to decide questions concerning candidates, strategies, and policies. The essence of the caucus idea, when applied to nominations, is that by sifting, sorting, and weeding out candidates prior to the election, leaders can assemble substantial support behind a single candidate, thus decreasing the prospect that the votes of like-minded citizens will be split among several candidates. Historically, the most important form of caucus was the *legislative caucus*, which was used successfully for the nomination of candidates for state and national offices, including the presidency, until 1824. The major drawback to the legislative caucus was that membership was limited to the party members in the legislature, thereby exposing the caucus to the charge that it was unrepresentative and undemocratic. A modest reform in the legislative caucus took place when provisions were made for seating delegates from districts held by the opposition party. Nevertheless, when the (Jeffersonian) Republican caucus failed to nominate Andrew Jackson for the presidency in 1824, it came under severe criticism from many quarters and shortly was abandoned.

Party Conventions   Advocates of reform in the nominating process turned to the party convention, already in use in some localities, as a substitute for the legislative caucus. The great merit of the convention system, it was argued, was that it could provide for representation, on a geographical basis, of all elements within the party. The secrecy of the caucus was displaced in favor of a more public arena, with nominations made by conventions composed of delegates drawn from various levels of the party organizations. As the convention method gained in prominence, so did the party organizations; state and local party leaders came to play a dominant role in the selection of candidates.

The convention system, however, failed to consolidate its early promise. Although it has been used for the nomination of presidential candidates from the 1830s to the present, it has given way to the direct primary for most other offices. Critics found that it suffered from essentially the same disabling properties as the caucus. In their view, it was sheer pretense to contend that the conventions were representative of the parties as a whole; rather they were run by party bosses without regard either for the views of the delegates or for the rules of fair play. An endless array of charges involving corruption in voting practices and procedures were made, and doubtless there was much truth in them. Growing regulation of conventions by the legislatures failed to assuage the doubts of the public. The direct primary came into favor as reformers came to understand its potential as a device for dismantling the structure of boss and "machine" influence and for introducing popular control over nominations.

The Direct Primary   Popular control of the political process has always been an important strand in the dogma of reformers. With its emphasis on voters rather than party organization, the direct primary was hard to resist; once Wisconsin adopted it for nomination of candidates for state elective offices in 1903, its use spread steadily throughout the country. Connecticut became the last state to adopt it, in 1955, but only after much tampering with the idea.[1] The Connecticut model (the "challenge" primary) combines convention and primary under an arrangement in which the party convention continues to make nominations, but with this proviso: if the party nominee at the convention is challenged by another candidate who receives as much as 20 percent of the convention votes, a primary must be held later. Otherwise, no primary is

---

[1] Despite its dominant position, the primary is not the exclusive method for making nominations in the states. In a few states conventions are still used to make nominations for certain statewide offices, such as governor or U.S. senator. Also, because competition for nominations within the Republican party in southern states is ordinarily not very great, the party is permitted to use conventions rather than primaries to make its nominations.

required, and the name of the convention nominee is automatically certified for the general election. The direct primary in Connecticut is something like a gun behind the door; on occasion there is resort to it. Ordinarily, however, the party organizations are not challenged, and convention decisions are final.

Part of the attractiveness of the primary is its apparent simplicity. From one perspective it is a device for transferring control over nominations from the party leadership to the rank-and-file voters; from another perspective it is a device for transferring control over nominating procedures from the party organization to the state. The primary rests on state law: it is an official election held at public expense, on a date set by the legislature, and supervised by public officials. It has often been interpreted as an attempt to institutionalize intraparty democracy.

It is not surprising that the direct primary has always had a better reception in reformist circles than anywhere else. For the party organization it poses problems rather than opportunities. Should the organization become involved in a contested primary for a major office, it is certain to have to raise large sums of money for the campaign of its candidate. If it remains neutral, it may wind up with a candidate who either is hostile to the organization or unsympathetic toward its programs and policies. Even if it abandons neutrality, there is no guarantee that its candidate will win; indeed, a good many political careers have been launched in primaries in which the nonendorsed candidate has convinced the voters that a vote for him is a vote to crush the "machine." Finally, the primary often works at cross purposes with the basic party objective of harmonizing its diverse elements by creating a "balanced" ticket for the general election. The voters are much less likely to nominate a "representative" slate of candidates, one that recognizes all major groups within the party, than the party leadership. Moreover, if the primary battle turns out to be bitter, the winner may enter the general election campaign with a sharply divided party behind him. It is no wonder that some political leaders have viewed the primary as a systematically conceived effort to bring down the party itself.

Types of Primaries

There are three basic types of primaries in use in the American states: closed, open, and blanket. Also in use among the states are three special forms of primaries: nonpartisan, run-off, and presidential (discussed in the next section).

Closed Primary The most common form of primary, in use in more than three-fourths of the states, is the closed primary. The key feature of this primary is that the voter may participate in the nomination of candidates only in the party to which he belongs. Ordinarily, in closed primary states, the voter is required to indicate his party affiliation at the time he registers to vote. This determines the party ballot he will be given at the primary election. Some states have a less rigorous requirement under which the voter merely reports his party affiliation at the time of the primary election and is given the ballot of that party. Where the tests of party membership are handled casually, there is some likelihood that voters cross over to participate in the selection of candidates of the other party.

Open Primary   From the point of view of the party organization, the open primary is less desirable than the closed primary. Used in nearly one-fourth of the states, the open primary poses no party membership requirements for the eligible voter. The voter may vote in the primary of any party. In the most common form of open primary, the voter is given the ballots of all parties, with instructions to vote for the candidates of one party and to discard the other ballots. There is nothing to prevent Democrats from voting to nominate Republican candidates or Republicans from voting to nominate Democratic candidates. Party leaders suffer from a special anxiety in open primary states: the possibility that voters of the competing party will "raid" their primary, hoping to nominate a weak candidate who would be easy to defeat in the general election. Whether "raiding" occurs with any frequency is difficult to say, but there is no doubt that in some states large numbers of voters cross over to vote in the other party's primary when an exciting contest is present. Probably the strongest appeal for the open primary is that it preserves the secrecy of the voter's party affiliation.

Blanket Primary   The state of Washington completes the circle of open primary states with what is known as a blanket primary. No primary is quite so open. Under its provisions the voter is given a ballot in which all candidates of all parties are listed under the separate offices. A voter may vote for a Democrat for one office and, responding to other impulses, vote for a Republican for another office. He cannot, of course, vote for more than one candidate for one office. The blanket primary is an invitation to "ticket splitting."

Nonpartisan Primary   In a number of states, judges, school board members, and other local government officials are selected in nonpartisan primaries. State legislators in Minnesota and Nebraska are also selected on this basis. The scheme itself is simple: the two candidates obtaining the greatest number of votes are nominated; in turn, they oppose each other in the general election. No party labels appear on the ballot in either election. The nonpartisan primary is defended on the grounds that partisanship should not be permitted to intrude upon the selection of certain officials, such as judges. By eliminating the party label, runs the assumption, the issues and divisiveness that dominate national and state party politics can be kept out of local elections and local offices. In point of fact, however, although nonpartisan primaries muffle the sounds of party, they do not eliminate them. It is not at all uncommon for the party organizations to slip quietly into the political process and to recruit and support candidates in these primaries; in such cases about all that is missing is the party label on the ballot.

Run-Off Primary   Another form of primary, the run-off or second primary, is a by-product of a one-party political environment. As used in southern states, this arrangement provides that if no candidate obtains a majority of the votes cast for that office, a run-off is held between the two leading candidates. The run-off primary is an attempt to come to terms with a chronic problem of a one-party system—essentially all competition is jammed into the primary of the dominant party. With numerous candidates seeking nomination for the same office, the vote is likely to be sharply split, with no candidate receiving a majority. A run-off between the top two candidates in the first primary provides a guarantee, if only statistical, that one candidate will emerge as the choice of a majority of voters. This is no small consideration in those southern states where the Democratic primary has long been the "real" election and where factionalism within the party has been so intense that no candidate would stand much of a chance of consolidating his party position without two primaries—the first to weed out the losers, and the second to endow the winner with the legitimacy a majority can offer.

An Overview of the Primary   In the perspectives of its early Progressive sponsors, the great virtue of the direct primary was its democratic component, its promise for changing the accent and scope of popular participation in the political system. Its immediate effect, it was hoped, would be to diminish the influence of political organization on political life. What is the evidence that the primary has accomplished its mission? What impact has it had on political party organization?

An important outcome of the primary is that it has served to sensitize party elites to the interests and feelings of rank-and-file members. Under the primary fewer nominations are "cut and dried." Even though candidates "slated" by the organization ordinarily go on to win the nomination, there is always some element of uncertainty over their prospects.[2] The possibility of a revolt against the organization, carried out in the primary, has forced party leaders to take careful account of the forces that constitute the party and to examine carefully the claims of potential candidates. As a result, intraparty relationships cannot as easily be taken for granted: there is always some chance that the aspirant who is overlooked by the party chieftains will decide to challenge their choice in the primary. The primary thus induces caution among party leaders. A "hands-off" policy—one in which the party makes no endorsement—is sometimes the party's only response. If it has no candidate, it cannot very well lose—some party leaders have been able to stay in business by avoiding the embarrassment that comes from primary defeats. In some jurisdictions the possibility of party intervention in the primary is never even seriously considered, so accustomed is the electorate to party-free contests. From the perspective of the public at large, it seems apparent that the main contribution of the primary is that it opens up the political process.

The primary has not immobilized party organizations, but it has caused a number of problems for them. It is not hard to understand party leaders' lack of enthusiasm for primaries when it is recognized that, among other things, the primary greatly increases party campaign costs (if the party backs a candidate in a contested primary), diminishes the capacity of the organization to reward its supporters through nominations, makes it difficult for the party to influence nominees who establish their own power bases in the primary electorate, creates the possibility that a person hostile to party leadership and party policies can capture a nomination, permits anyone to wear the party label and opens the possibility that the party will have to repudiate a candidate who has been thrust upon it, and increases intraparty strife and factionalism.[3] The imagination boggles at the thought of an institution better designed than the primary to stultify party organization and party processes.

Despite the pernicious effects that sometimes accompany the primary, the party has learned to live with it. This results, in part, from the failure of the primary to fulfill the expectations of its sponsors. Two things have gone awry. First, there has often been a lack of competitiveness in primaries. The surprising number of nominations that go by default may be due to any of several explanations. On the one hand, the lack of contested primaries may be evidence of party strength—that is, potential candidates stop short of entering the primary because their prospects appear slim for defeating the organization

---

[2] Laws in a few states make specific provisions for the parties to hold *preprimary conventions* for the purpose of choosing the "organization slate." The candidates selected by these conventions will usually appear on the ballot bearing the party endorsement. In the great majority of states, however, slating is an informal party process; the party depends on its organizational network and the communications media to inform the voters as to which candidates carry party support.

[3] These themes appear in Frank J. Sorauf, *Party Politics in America* (Boston: Little, Brown, 1968), pp. 210–211.

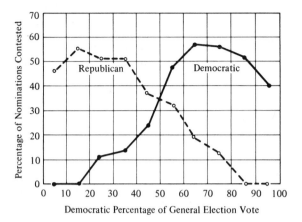

Figure 4
Primary Competition and the Prospects for General
Election Victory: Relation Between Proportion of
Nominations Contested and Percentage of General
Election Vote Polled by Republican and Democratic
Nominees for Missouri House of Representatives, 1942–1950

Source: V. O. Key, Jr., *American State Politics: An Introduction* (New York: Alfred A.
Knopf, Inc., 1956), p. 173.

choice. On the other hand, the "deserted" primary simply may testify to the
pragmatism of politicians: they do not struggle to win nominations that are
unlikely to lead anywhere. As V. O. Key, Jr., and others have shown, primaries
are most likely to be contested when the chances are strong that the winner
will be elected to office in the general election and least likely to be contested
when the nomination appears to have little value.[4] (See Figure 4.) The tendency is thus for competition to occur in competitive districts or in the
primary of the dominant party. Whatever the explanation, in this respect the
primary often bears little resemblance to its original design.

Second, experience with the primary has also shown that it is one thing to
shape an institution so as to induce popular participation and quite another
to realize it. No fact about primaries is more familiar than that large numbers
of voters assiduously ignore them. It is not at all uncommon for a majority of
voters to stay away from the polls on primary day, even when there are major
statewide races to be settled. What this means concretely is that the impact of
the wider public on the choice of candidates is minimized. The rule is starkly

---

[4] V. O. Key, Jr., *American State Politics: An Introduction* (New York: Knopf, 1956);
William H. Standing and James A. Robinson, "Inter-Party Competition and Primary
Contesting: The Case of Indiana," *American Political Science Review*, LII (December
1958), pp. 1066–1077; and Malcolm E. Jewell, "Party and Primary Competition in
Kentucky State Legislative Races," *Kentucky Law Journal*, XLVIII (Summer 1960),
pp. 517–535.

simple: when the turnout in primary elections is low, the probability is high that the "organization slate" will prevail. Although much of the public may pay little heed to primaries, a vigorous party will have little trouble turning out its workers and loyalists to support the party's choices. In a limited primary electorate the party organization wins far more often that it loses.

The National Convention

Probably the most remarkable institution in the world for making nominations is the American national nominating convention. Often sharply assailed, the convention functions today in generally the same fashion as it did in the middle of the nineteenth century. Undoubtedly students of politics could draw the blueprint for a more systematically constructed convention, but it is far from likely that they could design an institution that would better serve the political parties or better accommodate the interests that compose them. The great virtue of the national convention is that it presents an opportunity for the national party—the fifty state parties assembled—to come to terms with itself. Nowhere else in the political system is there a more logical place for state and national politicians to strike the necessary balances and to settle temporarily the continuing questions of leadership and policy.

The national convention is an outsized, unwieldy institution composed of more delegates than anyone really knows what to do with or where to lodge. Proposals to cut its size, usually suggested by outsiders, come up against the innate aversion of party professionals to any scheme that might threaten the party's efforts to build enthusiasm for the campaign. The theory of the party is quite simple on this point: the more local leaders or workers who can be involved in the convention (and implicated in its decisions), the greater the number of supporters who are likely to work on behalf of the presidential ticket. Moreover, a large convention serves an important function for state and local party leaders, since it enables them to name more delegates, and thus to pass out more benefits to those who have labored steadily in party vineyards. The large convention is therefore unlikely to be abandoned, however untidy it may appear. Consider these statistics on convention size: in 1968 there were 2,989 delegates and 2,512 alternates to the Democratic convention and 1,333 delegates and 1,333 alternates to the Republican convention. Such immoderate numbers call for a generalization. What seems to be suggested is that in the perspective of political leaders, administration never looms as important as politics.

The number of votes to be allocated to each state is established by the national committee through a formula based on two factors: the state's proportion of the electoral college vote and its contribution to the party's success in previous elections. The strength of individual states in the national convention will vary according to the formula that is utilized. For example, following a bitter dispute in the Democratic National Committee over the apportionment of delegates for the 1972 convention, a formula was accepted that increased the representation of large states (with large Democratic votes) at the expense of small states. Small states, especially those which have not voted strongly Democratic in presidential elections, would have preferred an apportionment formula based entirely on their electoral college strength.

Selection of Delegates—Party Committees, Conventions, and Primaries Historically, the apportionment of delegates has been a function of the national party, while provision for the selection of delegates has been left to the states. In a few states the choice of delegates is made by party state central committees. A majority of states select their delegates through some form of convention system. A common method is for some delegates to be chosen by congressional district conventions and the rest, by the party's state convention.

State processes for the selection of delegates in the Democratic party are now undergoing change. The 1970 report of the Commission on Party Structure and Delegate Selection established a number of selection guidelines to be followed by state Democratic parties, with a view to giving rank-and-file party members a "full, meaningful, and timely" opportunity to participate in the selection of delegates. When these changes have been implemented, the Democratic National Convention will be both more representative of the party as a whole and more responsive to its grass-roots elements.[5]

The best known and most controversial method for delegate selection is the presidential primary. Like the direct primary at the state level, the presidential primary was designed to wrest control over nominations from the "bosses" and to place it in the hands of the people by permitting them to choose the delegates to the presidential nominating conventions. The first state to employ this primary was Florida, beginning in 1904. In scarcely more than a decade nearly one-half of the states had adopted some version of it. Other states, however, found it difficult to break away from their familiar arrangements, and it was not long before the zeal supporting this reform was lost. Some states, which had eagerly adopted it, soon discarded it, returning to the older convention method. In 1968, only fifteen states and the District of Columbia held presidential primaries. Nonetheless, there has been a revival of interest in presidential primaries. Several states adopted presidential primary laws for 1972, bringing the total to twenty-two—the largest number since 1916.

---

[5] For a detailed examination of the Commission's guidelines, see the discussion in Chapter 6, pp. 155–158.

The diversity of state presidential primaries testifies to the fact that there is little agreement as to the best form. Each state, it seems, has added a distinctive touch to the presidential primary idea. Rather than exploring their uniqueness, it may be more useful to examine them in broad contour. Two principal types emerge. Under one arrangement voters are empowered to select delegates who, depending on state law, may or may not be bound to a particular candidate at the convention. Under the other form, the presidential preference primary, voters are given an opportunity to choose between the various candidates in the running for the party's presidential nomination. In effect, if no delegates are elected, the presidential preference primary turns out to be a popularity contest, leaving the winner uncertain as to how he will fare among the delegates chosen by the state convention. Finally, combining the two types, some states permit voters to choose delegates and also to express their preference for a presidential candidate.

The presidential primary system has achieved only modest success. Plainly, it has not revolutionized the nominating process, despite the fixed and steady optimism of the early reformers. What seems to have happened is that the primary simply has been absorbed by the convention system. Its contributions are at times important; at other times they are scarcely noticeable.

Evaluating Presidential Primaries   The criticisms leveled against the presidential primary system, as it now operates, cover immense ground. This primary, critics point out, occupies an anomalous position, at least in the public mind. Some variation of it is used in about forty percent of the states, while in the remainder the public has no direct influence on the choice of delegates and no opportunity to express a preference for any of the candidates. On occasion a single state's primary appears to govern the selection of the party's nominee. In the judgment of many observers, on the day that John F. Kennedy defeated Hubert H. Humphrey in the West Virginia presidential primary in 1960, he captured the Democratic nomination; at the same time, Humphrey's candidacy was finished.[6] In 1964 the critical Republican primary took place in California. In retrospect, it seems apparent that Barry Goldwater's narrow victory over Nelson Rockefeller in California assured his nomination, even though his performance in several earlier primaries had been disappointing. To the initiated voter, as well as the uninitiated, the presidential primary is a mass of oppositions and paradoxes in which one or a few states sometimes, but quite unpredictably, dominate the selection of a presidential nominee.

[6] The principal importance of the West Virginia primary for Kennedy was that it gave him an opportunity to convince apprehensive Democratic party leaders that his religion would not be a hindrance in the presidential campaign. By easily defeating Humphrey, a Protestant, in this overwhelmingly Protestant state, Kennedy sharply reduced the significance of the so-called Catholic issue.

There are other well-known difficulties associated with presidential primaries. Frequently the system is vitiated and undermined by the practice of the leading candidates of entering only those primaries that they think they have a good chance of winning, thereby diminishing the number of authentic contests.[7] In most presidential years there are only a few primaries with significant contests. Waging an extensive campaign in the primaries is also extraordinarily expensive; it has been estimated, for example, that in the 1968 California Democratic primary the forces of Robert Kennedy spent in excess of $2 million dollars while those supporting Eugene McCarthy spent about $1 million.[8] Just as the financial costs of campaigning are a heavy burden for candidates to bear, so also are the physical costs. The first primary comes as early as March, the last as late as mid-June, and there is scarcely any letup between them.

What plagues the presidential primary system above all else is simply the confusion that surrounds it. Perhaps the most confusion occurs in states in which the voters elect convention delegates and also choose among the presidential candidates (at least among those on the ballot). Although there are some states in which the delegates are bound to support the candidate who wins the preference vote, there are other states in which they are not. It is not uncommon for one candidate to win the preference poll and another candidate to capture a disproportionate share of the delegates to the convention. In still other states voters elect delegates but are not given any information on the ballot as to which presidential candidates they support. The practice of entering "favorite sons" in presidential primaries also tends to stultify the process and to confuse the voters; although it may serve the useful party function of holding the state delegation together and thereby improving its bargaining position in the convention, in no sense can the usual "favorite son" be considered an authentic candidate for the presidential nomination. And for the general run of voters, this ploy is likely to smack of chicanery.

Although the presidential primaries often create uncertainty and produce conflicting results, they should not be explained only in these terms. They do give rank-and-file party voters a larger role in the presidential nominating process. Moreover, they present an opportunity for testing candidacies and policies in at least some states. It would be difficult to exaggerate the importance of the Democratic primaries in 1968, all but one of which were won by either Senator Eugene McCarthy or Senator Robert Kennedy in campaigns

---

[7] Although candidates take calculated risks concerning which primaries to enter, there are a few which they cannot avoid. For example, the secretary of state of Oregon is empowered to place the names of all generally recognized aspirants for the presidential nomination on the primary ballot; any person selected in this process can have his name removed from the ballot if he certifies that he is not a candidate for the nomination.

[8] *The New York Times*, June 3, 1969, p. 41.

that challenged the Johnson Administration and mobilized support against his policies, particularly that of Vietnam.[9] Indeed, a major reason advanced for President Johnson's decision not to seek reelection was the intensity and the success of the preconvention challenge launched by Senator McCarthy and Senator Kennedy. There is merit to the argument that even though only a minority of states hold presidential primaries, the press and television coverage they receive permits the nation as a whole to become familiar with the candidates and to take their measure as potential Presidents.

The need for some form of popular endorsement impels many presidential candidates to test their appeal in the primaries. But there are great dangers in doing so. It is clear that John F. Kennedy's string of victories in the primaries in 1960, more than anything else, led to his nomination. Numerous state and local Democratic leaders would have preferred a "safer" candidate, but they found it impossible to withstand the surge of public support behind Kennedy. Something of the same story explains Dwight D. Eisenhower's victory over Robert A. Taft in 1952. Nevertheless, it seems evident that the primaries are about as likely to terminate candidacies as to promote them. Hubert H. Humphrey's loss to John F. Kennedy in West Virginia in 1960 took him out of the race as did Nelson Rockefeller's loss to Barry Goldwater in California in 1964. The several primary defeats inflicted on Eugene McCarthy by Robert Kennedy undoubtedly damaged McCarthy's prospects for upsetting Humphrey in the 1968 convention. The list could easily be extended. Despite the risks that attend the candidates' decisions to enter the presidential primaries, it is no longer easy to avoid them—at least not all of them. An important reason for entering the primaries is simply one of statistics: over half of the delegates are chosen by this method. The candidate who elects to concentrate his campaign on key party leaders and the delegates to be chosen by state conventions and party committees, rather than to face the voters in the primaries, may find that by the time the convention gets under way the nomination has already been "sewed up" by a candidate who can claim to be the "peoples' choice."

The Convention Delegates   Some myths about American politics and political institutions are difficult to put to rest. Consider the delegates to the national conventions. The traditional evaluation of the delegates commonly pictured them as men of modest talents and frequently tarnished reputations. To make matters worse, they were usually thought to be under the thumb of local bosses, their votes easily bartered for one or another kind of favor. How

---

[9] President Johnson won a narrow victory over Senator McCarthy in the presidential preference poll in New Hampshire, but McCarthy won twenty of the twenty-four convention delegates.

true this representation may have been during the reformist era in the early twentieth century is hard to say, but it scarcely appears accurate today. The salient facts about delegates in recent conventions is that many have been highly successful, even prestigious, politicians and that, by and large, they have not resembled a cross section of the population. The typical delegate has a college education and earns an income much above that of the average American citizen. Lawyers, businessmen, and other professions are heavily represented among the state delegations. Neither Negroes nor women, on the other hand, have representation in proportion to their numbers in the population.[10] Conspicuous in most state delegations are well-known and experienced public officials, including governors, mayors, and members of Congress and the Cabinet. The important point to recognize is that a great many delegates have had substantial experience with decision-making in public, party, and private institutions of all kinds. The power they hold in their own right requires party leaders to take them seriously and contributes to a leader-follower relationship characterized more by negotiation, persuasion, and bargaining than by management and manipulation.[11]

The Politics of the Convention

Three practical aims dominate the proceedings of the national convention: to nominate presidential and vice-presidential candidates, to draft the party platform, and to lay the groundwork for party unity in the campaign. The way in which the party addresses itself to the tasks of drafting the platform and nominating the candidates is likely to determine how well it achieves its third objective, that of healing party rifts and forging a cohesive party. To put together a platform and a presidential ticket that satisfies the principal elements of the party is exceedingly difficult. It is not unusual for some delegates, unhappy over the turn of events, either to walk out of the convention—as some southern state delegations have done in recent Democratic Conventions —or else to "sit out" the campaign. The task of reconciling divergent interests

[10] The situation is changing rapidly, however, in terms of black representation. Although only 2.2 percent of the delegates to the 1964 Democratic Convention were blacks, the percentage grew to 6.1 in 1968. Black delegates are always more numerous in the Democratic Convention than in the Republican. For data on black representation in Democratic state delegations in 1968, see the *Congressional Quarterly Weekly Report*, August 23, 1968, p. 2244.

[11] See Karl O'Lessker, "State Delegations, Leaders and Followers," in Paul Tillett (ed.), *Inside Politics: The National Conventions, 1960* (Dobbs Ferry, N.Y.: Oceana Publications, 1962), pp. 170–180. For a discussion of the factors that affect the individual delegate's freedom of action, see Donald B. Johnson, "Delegate Selection for National Conventions," in Cornelius P. Cotter (ed.), *Practical Politics in the United States* (Boston: Allyn and Bacon, 1969), pp. 225–228.

within the party occupies the convention from its earliest moments until the final gavel. By and large, convention leaders have been remarkably successful in shaping the compromises necessary to keep the national party, such as it is, from flying apart.

The Convention Committees   The initial business of the convention is handled mainly by four committees. The *committee on credentials* is given the responsibility for determining the permanent roll (official membership) of the convention. Its specific function is to ascertain the members' legal right to seats in the convention. In the absence of challenges to the right of certain delegates to be seated or contests between two delegations from the same state, each trying to be seated, the review is handled routinely and with dispatch. Most state delegations are seated without difficulty. When disputes arise, the committee holds hearings and takes testimony; its recommendations for seating delegates are then reported to the convention, where ordinarily (but not invariably) they are sustained.[12] The *committee on permanent organization* is charged with the responsibility of selecting the permanent officers of the convention, including the permanent chairman, the clerks, and the sergeant at arms. The *committee on rules* devises the rules under which the convention will operate and establishes the order of business.

Ordinarily the most important of the convention committees is the *committee on resolutions*, which is in charge of the drafting of the party platform. The actual work of this committee begins many weeks in advance of the convention, so that usually there is a draft of the document by the time the convention opens and the formal committee hearings begin. When a President seeks reelection, the platform is likely to be prepared under his direction and accepted by the committee (and later by the floor) without major changes. The struggle over the nomination may influence the drafting of the platform, since the leading candidates have a vested interest in securing planks that are compatible with their views. Indeed, the outcomes of clashes over planks

---

[12] Some conventions have an uncommon number of credentials disputes. In the 1968 Democratic Convention, for example, fifteen state delegations were challenged in whole or in part. Several different issues were involved. A number of southern state delegations came under review for having alleged racial imbalance and also for having delegates of dubious loyalty to the party. Several northern state delegations were challenged on the grounds that the delegate selection process was improper, with the result that certain state factions had no representation in the delegation. And still other state delegations were attacked for their failure to reflect their state's political sentiments toward the leading candidates. In only one instance did the credentials committee decide wholly in favor of the challengers. In the case of Mississippi the committee voted to seat the Loyal National Democrats, a biracial group, instead of the regular state party delegation. In the Georgia case the committee voted to seat both the regular state delegation and the challengers, splitting the state's votes between them. See the *Congressional Quarterly Weekly Report*, August 23, 1968, pp. 2242–2245, and August 30, 1968, p. 2286.

frequently provide a good indication of which candidate will capture the nomination. In the 1968 Democratic Convention, for example, it was all but certain that Hubert H. Humphrey would win the nomination when the convention, after a lengthy and emotional floor debate, adopted by a comfortable margin a plank that reflected the Johnson Administration's position on the war in Vietnam. His two principal opponents, Senators Eugene J. McCarthy and George S. McGovern, were the most prominent supporters of the losing (committee) minority plank, which called for an unconditional halt to the bombing of North Vietnam.

Selecting the Presidential Ticket   The principal task with which the convention must come to terms is the selection of the presidential nominee. Only a few candidates, in any real sense, are ever in the running for this office. The candidates who come under serious consideration, whose names are bruited about in the convention hall and in the hotel rooms of the convention city, are those who best meet the tests of "availability"—that is, who possess certain qualities that set them apart from other men and make them especially attractive as candidates for the presidency. The availability rules have never been hard and fast, though they have tended to favor candidates whose backgrounds revealed these characteristics: rural or small-town origins, Anglo-Saxon descent, Protestant faith, happy family life, successful political career (particularly as governor), and residence in a large, northern state. Although a surprising number of earlier presidential candidates have qualified on these tests of political feasibility, there are some signs that such tests are undergoing redefinition. Consider, for example, those that relate to the candidate's religion and career. The rule of Protestantism has now been breached twice by the Democratic convention, in 1928 when Al Smith was nominated and in 1960 when John F. Kennedy was nominated. Similarly, the rule that favors governors seems to be of lessening significance. All the candidates in the presidential elections of the 1960s—Kennedy and Nixon, Johnson and Goldwater, Humphrey and Nixon—came into prominence as U.S. senators rather than as governors.

The availability rules change over time, not because the parties engage in steady introspection, but because they are careful monitors of the changing political universe and of changing popular attitudes. Party professionals have an acute sense of where the best opportunities lie for victory. Following the elementary rule of all politics, they support candidates who they think can meet popular expectations and, therefore, who can win.

To at least some party leaders, the best convention is one that opens with significant uncertainties and imponderables—a good, though not surefire, prescription for generating public interest in the convention, the party, and its nominees. In the usual convention, however, uncertainties are far from numerous. Doubts are much more likely to surround the choice of the vice-presidential nominee than the presidential nominee. So many presidential candidates are screened out in the months of preconvention maneuvering that by the time the convention opens the range of choice has become sharply narrowed, perhaps nonexistent. Consider recent conventions. In both the 1960 and 1968 Republican Conventions, Richard M. Nixon's nomination occurred on the first ballot, without really significant opposition. In 1964, in the judgment of most party professionals, Barry Goldwater's nomination was assured by his victory over Nelson Rockefeller in the California primary. The great bulk of the Goldwater delegates had been captured earlier in state conventions. The Democratic experience is about the same. Lyndon Johnson's nomination in 1964 was a foregone conclusion, following the custom that incumbent Presidents are entitled to a second term if they choose to run. In 1968, with the forces opposed to the Johnson Administration in disarray following the assassination of Robert F. Kennedy, there was scarcely any doubt but that Hubert H. Humphrey would emerge as the party standard-bearer.

The stark fact is that in only a few conventions in the last two decades has there been substantial doubt about the ultimate winner: both conventions in 1952 (Eisenhower vs. Taft in the Republican Convention and a wide-open contest in the Democratic Convention) and the Democratic Convention in 1960 (John F. Kennedy, who won the presidential primaries, vs. the field). In recent years the "front runner"—the candidate holding the most delegate votes prior to the convention—has gone on to victory, winning nomination on the first ballot.

The final major item of convention business is the selection of the party's vice-presidential nominee. Here the task of the party is to come up with the right political formula—the candidate who can add the most to the ticket and detract the least. In all but rare cases the presidential nominee makes the choice himself, following rounds of consultation with various party leaders.[13] Although a great deal of suspense is usually created over the vice-presidential nomination, convention ratification comes easily once the presidential nominee has made up his mind and "cleared" the selection with key leaders. Unless the presidential nominee is inclined to take a major risk to serve the interest of his own faction or ideology (as Barry Goldwater did in choosing Republican National Chairman William E. Miller in 1964), he selects a candidate

---

[13] An exception to this "rule" occurred in 1956 when Adlai Stevenson, the Democratic presidential nominee, created a stir by declining to express a preference for his vice-presidential running mate. Left to its own devices, the convention quickly settled on a choice between Senators Estes Kefauver and John F. Kennedy. Kefauver, who had been an active candidate for the presidency, won a narrow victory. Kennedy came off even better—he launched his candidacy for the presidential nomination in 1960.

who can help to balance the ticket and unify the party.[14] The range of his choice, of course, may be constricted by the necessity for rewarding a particular party element (for example, sectional or ideological), the support of which was critical to his own nomination.

Appraising the National Convention   The salience of value and taste are nowhere more apparent than in the evaluations made of the national convention. The facts of the convention are the same, or essentially the same, for all who observe the institution, but the conclusions drawn as to its merits are often diametrically opposite. To spear all the stray appraisals of the convention—worse yet to consider them—would be a task of major proportions, so much has been written about this controversial institution. The following evaluations may be sufficient to show the main paths along which the arguments have moved:

> The average delegate never knows what is going on. The hall is in dreadful confusion, and the speeches from the platform are mainly irrelevant and unintelligible. The real business is done under the stage, in dark and smelly rooms, or in hotel suites miles away.[15]

> In my opinion—and I think most Americans will agree—our Presidential nominating conventions have become a thoroughly disgraceful spectacle which can scarcely fail to appall our own voters and create a shockingly bad image of our country abroad.[16]

> The national political convention as we have known it is a messy, obsolete, and thoroughly unsatisfying way of selecting a candidate for the Presidency of the United States. . . . The political convention as we have known it is no longer acceptable. It is in sharp conflict with the growing importance of the primary election and will have to yield to it before it seriously disfigures the democratic process and American society itself.[17]

> The national party conventions are . . . a vital part of the American political system. Smoke-filled rooms are indispensable to their successful operation. . . . The only real alternative to the convention system is a nation-wide presi-

[14] The preference of party professionals for a balanced ticket grows out of their instinct for the conservation of the party and their understanding of the electorate. The ticket should be broadly appealing, in their view, rather than narrowly ideological or sectional. The factors that ordinarily come under review in the consideration of balance are geography, political philosophy, religion, and factional recognition.

[15] H. L. Mencken, "What is Going On in the World?," *American Mercury,* June 1932, p. 138.

[16] Dwight D. Eisenhower, "Our National Nominating Conventions Are a Disgrace," *Reader's Digest,* July 1966, p. 76.

[17] Norman Cousins, "The Breakdown of Political Conventions," *Saturday Review,* September 14, 1968, p. 30. Copyright 1968 by Saturday Review, Inc.

dential primary system. . . . The difficulties with such a system are two fold. It would not guarantee an end to "boss control"; experience with primaries has proved that party organizations often can dominate primary elections as easily as they dominate conventions. More important, primary elections on a national scale could disrupt party solidarity and effectiveness.[18]

The great merit of the convention system is that in its search for the winning candidate it tends to discard the extremists and bring forward the men around whom not only the party but the nation as well may best rally.[19]

The convention . . . is an essential part of the American System. It has rendered far more good service than it has done harm, and no really effective substitute for it has been suggested. For the conventions do something that no other organ of the American system of democracy does: they provide a meeting place for a representative sample of all types of politicians, amateur and professional; they supply, however imperfectly, one great need of the American system, the nationalizing of party politics, and they are a substitute for a missing class in American political life, a group of universally recognized national political leaders. They are, in fact, a consequence of the separation of powers and of the federal system. If the presidency were subordinate to Congress or if great political careers could be made only nationally, the conventions would not be necessary. As it is, they are.[20]

Political Campaigns

It is difficult to bring political campaigns into articulate focus for one very good reason: campaigns come in an extraordinary variety of shapes and sizes. Whether there is such a thing as a typical campaign is open to serious doubt. It seems clear, for example, that campaigns will differ depending upon the office sought (whether executive, legislative, or judicial), the level of government (national, state, or local), the legal and political environments (partisan or nonpartisan election, competitive or noncompetitive constituency), and the initial advantages or disadvantages of the candidates (incumbent or nonincumbent, well-known or little-known), among other things.

The standards by which to measure and evaluate the effectiveness of campaigns are not easy to discover because of the vast number of variables that intrude both on campaign decisions and on voter choice. In the usual election, does the party that wins owe its victory to a superior campaign or

[18] James McGregor Burns, "The Case for the Smoke-Filled Room," *New York Times Magazine,* June 15, 1952, pp. 9, 25. © 1952/61/70 by The New York Times Company. Reprinted by permission.

[19] Paul H. Douglas, "Conventions and the Popular Will," *The New Republic,* March 28, 1955, p. 14. Reprinted by permission of the New Republic © 1955, 70, Harrison-Blaine of New Jersey, Inc.

[20] D. W. Brogan, *Politics in America,* New York: Harper & Row, Publishers, Inc., 1954, p. 234.

would it have won in any case? Data with which to answer such a question obviously are elusive. What is evident is that strategies that are appropriate to one campaign may be less appropriate or even inappropriate to another. Tactics that work at one time or in one place may not work at another time or in another place. Organizational arrangements that satisfy one party may not satisfy the other. Campaigns, in a word, are loaded with imponderables. There are numerous factors over which neither the party organizations nor the candidates have any control. Moreover, there is no way for parties and candidates to develop an immunity against campaign mistakes. Even so, in most cases it is not immediately clear when a miscalculation has been made, how serious it may have been, or how best to restore the damage.

Despite the variability and uncertainty that characterize political campaigns, there are a few general requirements imposed upon all candidates and parties. The candidate making a serious bid for votes must acquire certain resources and meet certain problems. Whatever his perspective of the campaign, he will have to come to terms with matters of organization, strategy, and finances.

Campaign Organization   Very likely the single most important fact to be known about campaign organization is that the regular party organizations are ill-equipped by themselves to organize and conduct campaigns. Of necessity, they look to outsiders for assistance in all kinds of party work and for the development and staffing of auxiliary campaign organizations. In major campaigns there are a multiplicity of organizational units engaged in the collection and expenditure of funds and in the development and execution of campaign plans. For example, in the 1968 presidential election there were ninety-seven separate campaign committees that reported national-level expenditures on behalf of the Democratic ticket, including such groups as Advertising Executives for Humphrey-Muskie, Businessmen for Humphrey-Muskie, Citizens for Humphrey-Muskie, County Officials for Humphrey-Muskie, Educators for Humphrey-Muskie, Independents for Humphrey-Muskie, Lawyers for Humphrey-Muskie, Pharmacists for Humphrey-Muskie, and Rural Electric Americans for Humphrey-Muskie.[21] The national organizations, of course, are but the tip of the iceberg. State and local citizens units of great variety are also created, each with its own leaders, supporters, and sources of money. At times these groups work in impressive harmony with the regular party organizations (perhaps to the point of being wholly dominated by them), and at other times they function as virtually independent units, seemingly oblivious to the requirements for communication or for coordination of their activities with those of other party or auxiliary units.

[21] *1969 Congressional Quarterly Almanac*, p. 2443.

The regular party organizations share control of campaigns not only with the citizens groups but also with a variety of political action committees that operate under the sponsorship of certain interest groups. Among the best known of these groups are the AFL-CIO Committee on Political Education (COPE), the American Medical Association Political Action Committee, and the National Committee for an Effective Congress. Like other campaign groups, these committees raise campaign funds, endorse candidates, and otherwise support those candidates in sympathy with their positions and programs.

At the top of the heterogeneous cluster of party and auxiliary campaign committees are the campaign organizations created by the individual candidates. Virtually every candidate for an important, competitive office feels it obligatory to develop his personal campaign organization to counsel him on strategy and issues, to assist him with travel arrangements and speeches, to raise money, to defend his interests in party circles, and to try to coordinate his activities with those of other candidates and campaign units. The size of the candidate's personal organization is likely to vary according to the significance of the office and the competitiveness of the constituency. The congressman from a safe district, for example, habituated to easy elections, scarcely needs either an organization or a campaign. Indeed, some congressional districts are so safe that were it not for certain district party rites that the incumbent is obligated to attend, he could easily skip campaigning and remain in Washington.

In some campaigns the regular party organization is reduced to being just another spectator. It is not unusual for candidates to employ professional management firms to direct their campaigns rather than to rely on the party organizations. All facets of American politics today come under the influence of public relations specialists and advertising firms. Possessing resources which the party organizations cannot match, they raise funds, recruit campaign workers, develop issues, gain endorsements, write speeches, arrange campaign schedules, direct the candidate's television appearances, and prepare campaign literature, films, and advertising. Indeed, they sometimes create the overall campaign strategy and dominate day-to-day decision-making. Put baldly, their principal task is to build the candidate's "image" by controlling the way he appears to the general public. The observations of one of Richard M. Nixon's campaign advisers in the 1968 presidential election make the point:

> [Nixon] has to come across as a person larger than life, the stuff of legend. People are stirred by legend, including the living legend, not by the man himself. It's the aura that surrounds the charismatic figure more than it is the figure itself that draws the followers. Our task is to build that aura. . . .[22]

[22] Quoted by Joe McGinniss, *The Selling of the President, 1968.* © 1969 by Joemac, Incorporated. Reprinted by permission of Trident Press/division of Simon & Schuster, Inc.

Campaign Strategy The paramount goal of all major party campaigns is to bring together a coalition of sufficient size to bring victory to the candidate or party. Ordinarily the early days of the campaign are devoted to the development and testing of a broad campaign strategy designed to produce a winning coalition. In the most general sense, strategy should be seen as "an overall plan for acquiring and using the resources needed for a campaign."[23] In developing a broad strategy, candidates, their advisors, and party leaders must take into consideration a number of factors. These include the principal themes to be developed during the campaign, the issues to be emphasized and exploited, the candidate's personal qualities to be emphasized, the specific groups and geographical areas to whom appeals will be directed, the acquisition of financial support and endorsements, the timing of campaign activities, the relationship of the candidate to the party organization and to factions within it, and the uses to be made of the communications media, particularly television.

To the casual observer, it may appear that there are no limits to the number of major and minor strategies open to a resourceful candidate. In point of fact, however, there are a number of important constraints that serve to shape and define the candidate's options. It is reasonable to expect, for example, that campaign strategy will be affected by the political, social, and economic environments that are present. Among these factors which intrude on campaign strategy are the competitiveness of the district, the nature of the electorate, the quality and representativeness of the party ticket, the unity of the party, the presence of an incumbent, the election timetable (for example, presidential or off-year election), and the predispositions and commitments of political interest groups. And though it is difficult to weigh its significance, it seems clear that the temper of the times will also affect the candidate's broad plan of action. "In eras of general complacency and economic well-being," V. O. Key has written, "assaults against the interests and crusades against abuses by the privileged classes seem to pay small dividends. Periods of hardship and unrest move campaigners to contrive strategies to exploit the anxieties of people—or to insulate themselves from public wrath."[24] Whatever the impact of these constraints upon campaign strategy, it seems evident that most of them are beyond the control of the candidate; they are, pure and simple, conditions to which he must adjust and adapt. The overall

[23] David A. Leuthold, *Electioneering in a Democracy* (New York: Wiley, 1968), p. 3. Leuthold's study of congressional campaigns shows that "the problems of acquisition are more significant than the problems of using the resources. As a result, the decision on making an appeal for the labor vote, for example, will depend not only on the proportion of the constituency which is labor-oriented, but also on the success that the candidate has had in acquiring such resources as the support of labor leaders, the money and workers needed to send a mailing to labor union members, and information about issues important to labor people."

[24] V. O. Key, *Politics, Parties, & Pressure Groups*, p. 464.

strategy that the candidate fashions or selects must be consonant with the "givens" of the campaign environment.

Opportunities and constraints vary from campaign to campaign and from candidate to candidate. Although this results in great diversity, it is nevertheless possible to depict the three overarching strategies that all serious candidates follow. The most important is for the candidate to *get his supporters out to vote.* A great many elections are won or lost depending on the turnout of the party faithful. In fact, there is good reason to believe that minority party candidates would win most elections if all they were to accomplish was to increase the rate of turnout of their own supporters (assuming turnout for the major party candidates remained the same). The second general strategy is to *activate latent support.* Successful campaigns often turn on the ability of the candidate to activate potential voters among those groups that ordinarily support his party. For the Democratic candidate this means that special effort must be directed to activating such segments of the population as Catholics, Jews, Negroes, blue-collar workers, union members, and urban residents; for the Republican candidate this rule prescribes a similar effort to activate Protestants, whites, suburban and rural residents, and professional, business, and managerial elements. The third general strat-

"How many times have you asked yourself, 'What can *I*, as a single person, possibly do to help shape the destiny of mankind? Well, I'll tell you what you can do. You can vote for me."

Drawing by D. Fradon; © 1968 The New Yorker Magazine, Inc.

egy is to *change the opposition.* This strategy on occasion has been spectacularly successful. A large number of Democrats, for example, voted for Dwight D. Eisenhower in the elections of 1952 and 1956, and a large number of Republicans bolted their party to vote for Lyndon B. Johnson in 1964. Ordinarily, this is the least promising of the three strategies. With limited resources at his disposal, the typical candidate is more likely to be elected by getting his supporters and latent supporters to the polls than by trying to convert members of the other party. The important point is that strategies—particularly those relating to manipulation of symbols and issues—will vary sharply according to the audience to whom appeals are directed.[25]

Myths and facts are mixed in about equal proportion in the lore of campaign strategy. Strategies are not easily devised, sorted out, or tested. Indeed, it is scarcely ever apparent in advance which strategies are likely to be most productive and which least productive or even counter-productive. However disciplined and well-managed campaigns may appear to those who stand on the outskirts, they rarely are in reality. As Stimson Bullitt has observed:

> A politician, unlike a general or an athlete, never can be invincible, except within a constituency which constitutes a sinecure. Furthermore, a candidate cannot even be sure that his campaigning will change the election result. . . . [A] politician must act on his hypotheses, which are tested only by looking backward on his acts. A candidate cannot even experiment. Because no one knows what works in a campaign, money is spent beyond the point of diminishing returns. To meet similar efforts of the opposition all advertising and propaganda devices are used—billboards, radio, TV, sound trucks, newspaper ads, letter writing or telephone committee programs, handbills, bus cards. No one dares to omit any approach. Every cartridge must be fired because among the multitude of blanks one may be a bullet. . . .

> A common mistake of post-mortems is to assert that a certain event or a stand or mannerism of a candidate caused him to win or lose. Often no one knows whether the election result was because of this factor or despite it. Spectacular events, whether a dramatic proposal, an attack, or something in the news outside the campaign, are like a revolving door. They win some voters and lose others. . . .[26]

The evidence of many studies suggests that campaign decisions are about as likely to be shaped by chance and by the ability of the candidate to seize upon events as they are by the careful formulation of a broad and coherent

[25] Lewis A. Froman, Jr., "A Realistic Approach to Campaign Strategies and Tactics," in M. Kent Jennings and L. Harmon Zeigler (eds.) *The Electoral Process* (Englewood Cliffs, N.J.: Prentice-Hall, 1966), pp. 7–8.

[26] Stimson Bullitt, *To Be a Politician* (Garden City, N.Y.: Doubleday, 1961), pp. 72–73.

plan of attack. Consider the decision of John F. Kennedy in the 1960 presidential campaign to telephone Mrs. Martin Luther King to express his concern over the welfare of her husband, who had been jailed in Atlanta following a "sit in" in a department store. There is no evidence that Kennedy's decision—perhaps as critical as any of the campaign—was based upon a comprehensive assessment of alternatives or possible consequences. Rather, according to Theodore H. White, the decision came about in this way:

> The crisis was instantly recognized by all concerned with the Kennedy campaign. . . . [The] suggestion for meeting it [was made by] Harris Wofford. Wofford's idea was as simple as it was human—that the candidate telephone directly to Mrs. King in Georgia to express his concern. Desperately Wofford tried to reach his own chief, Sargent Shriver, head of the Civil Rights Section of the Kennedy campaign, so that Shriver might break through to the candidate barnstorming somewhere in the Middle West. Early [the next] morning, Wofford was able to locate Shriver . . . and Shriver enthusiastically agreed. Moving fast, Shriver reached the candidate [as he] was preparing to leave for a day of barnstorming in Michigan. The candidate's reaction to Wofford's suggestion of participation was impulsive, direct, and immediate. From his room at the Inn, without consulting anyone, he placed a long-distance telephone call to Mrs. Martin Luther King, assured her of his interest and concern in her suffering and, if necessary, his intervention. . . . The entire episode received only casual notice from the generality of American citizens in the heat of the last three weeks of the Presidential campaign. But in the Negro community the Kennedy intervention rang like a carillon.[27]

Campaign Money   Of all the requirements for successful campaigns, perhaps none is more important than a strong infusion of money. Campaign costs have risen steadily over the years. In 1952, for example, expenditures for the nomination and election of public officials at all levels of government came to about $140 million. In 1956, costs rose to perhaps $155 million, in 1960, to about $175 million, and in 1964, to roughly $200 million. For 1968, estimates suggest that at least $300 million was spent on politics at all levels. The spiraling costs of running for office are caused by a number of factors. The steady increase in the general price level is, of course, one reason. To this must be added the costs that have accompanied utilization of new techniques in campaigning (particularly television), the growth in population, and the enlargement of the electorate. Whether campaign money is

[27] From *The Making of the President, 1960* by Theodore H. White. Copyright © 1961 by Atheneum House, Inc. Reprinted by permission of the author and Atheneum Publishers, pp. 322–323. For analysis of the major models of campaign decision-making, see Karl A. Lamb and Paul A. Smith, *Campaign Decision-Making: The Presidential Election of 1964* (Belmont, Calif.: Wadsworth Publishing Company, 1968).

spent intelligently is impossible to say. Candidates spend as heavily as they do because neither they nor their advisers know which expenditures are likely to produce the greatest return in votes. Lacking systematic information, they jump at every opportunity to contact and persuade the voters—and every opportunity costs money.

So many different party and nonparty groups are engaged in the collection and expenditure of campaign funds at all levels of government that it is virtually impossible to make comprehensive statements about the sources of money or its disposition. A few general observations must suffice.[28] At the national level both parties customarily receive most of their funds in large contributions (sums of $500 or more). Fund-raising dinners ($100-a-plate) are a particularly lucrative source of campaign money; in 1964–1965, for example, nearly $10 million was pledged at fund-raising events attended by President Johnson. The major parties have also developed quota systems under which each state party is expected to contribute a certain sum to the support of the national party. Large sums of money have been produced by groups such as the Democrat's "President's Club" and the Republican's "Associates," with membership in each reserved for those individuals who contribute at least $1,000 to the campaign. The parties have recently attempted to increase the proportion of money received in small amounts by developing such programs as the Republican's Neighbor to Neighbor campaign and the Democrat's Dollars for Democrats; nevertheless, it is probable that 90 percent of all political money is contributed by less than 10 percent of the population.

There are four principal categories of campaign expenditures: general overhead (maintenance of campaign headquarters and staff), field activity (meetings, rallies, and travel), publicity (newspaper advertising and radio and television advertising and programs), and election day expenses (stipends for election day workers, and so on.) At the national level expenditures for radio and television broadcasts are especially heavy—a 30-minute network television program, for example, may cost $100,000 simply for air time.[29]

Individuals contribute to political campaigns for a variety of reasons. There are undoubtedly some contributors who give money out of a sense of civic duty or for the psychological satisfaction they receive from assisting

[28] This section draws particularly on the work of Herbert E. Alexander, "The Cost of Presidential Elections," in Cornelius P. Cotter (ed.), *Practical Politics in the United States*, pp. 277–315.

[29] According to estimates by the Federal Communications Commission, expenditures for political broadcasts on television and radio grew from about $10 million in 1956 to $40 million in 1968—an increase of 400 percent in only 12 years. See the 1969 *Congressional Quarterly Almanac*, p. 2442 and the report, *Financing a Better Election System* (New York: Committee for Economic Development, 1968), p. 16.

their party or a particular candidate. Very probably there are far more contributors who donate to campaign coffers because they want to elect candidates of suitable ideological bent and because they hope to influence the course of public policy. What kinds of benefits accrue to those individuals who pay the costs of political campaigns? Is there in any sense a "payoff"? Alexander Heard, a leading expert on campaign finance, argues as follows:

> . . . What contributors buy is not as tangible as is often supposed. Mostly what they buy is "access." Politicians who get the money, along with solicitors who raise it and contributors themselves, state invariably that in return for his funds a contributor can get, if he seeks it, access to the party, legislative or administrative officials concerned with a matter of interest to him. One lobbyist called it "entree" and another called it "a basis for talking." Access may not give the contributor what he wants, as the number of disgruntled (and talkative) contributors indicates. And if he is eligible for what he wants, a government contract or a job, he will often get it anyway. The main result of access, said a former national treasurer noted for his persuasion with the fatter cats, is to "speed things up." The number of cold bargains that are struck for campaign funds are negligible. The real influence derived from big contributions is a latent one, derived through access. This access can be obtained through any sort of political service, and many politicians argue stoutly that campaign work at the right level produces greater influence than money. But large contributions pave a sure road to the decision-making centers of government for those who want to present their case, which is often all they need, and this consequence of our way of financing elections looms as far more significant than the difference in the volume of funds available to the parties.[30]

Campaign Finance: The Need for Reform   Public uneasiness over the role of money in American politics has long been present. Dissatisfaction traces from two main complaints. The first is simply that campaign costs have risen to such an extent that candidates with limited resources are seriously disadvantaged in the electoral process.[31] The doubt persists that some men of talent never become candidates for public office because they lack financial support or are unwilling to solicit funds from others because of the risk of

[30] Alexander Heard, *Money and Politics* (New York: Public Affairs Pamphlet No. 242, 1956), p. 15.

[31] A rough notion of the enormity of campaign spending by individual candidates may be gleaned from expenditure estimates for certain 1970 primaries. A Republican candidate for the U.S. Senate nomination in California reportedly spent $1,900,000 in an unsuccessful bid for the office. Not far behind, a Democratic candidate for the U.S. Senate in New York spent $1,800,000, and a Democratic candidate for governor of Pennsylvania spent $1,200,000. Both won. It is important to emphasize that these sums were spent simply in contested primaries. Expenditures in the general elections in these states undoubtedly ran higher. *Congressional Quarterly Weekly Report*, August 14, 1970, p. 2061.

"They say to get elected to public office in America one must be rich. Well, my friends, *I'm* rich. I'm *very* rich."

Drawing by Dana Fradon; © 1970 The New Yorker Magazine, Inc.

incurring political indebtedness and of compromising their independence.[32] Moreover, the high cost of elections sometimes means that the public hears only one side of the campaign, that of the candidate with access to "real" money. The second complaint is that those individuals, families, and groups

---

[32] Some members of Congress are acutely aware of the problem of rising campaign costs. A New York congressman observes: "When I ran for Congress, the first question asked me was whether I could finance my own campaign. If I had said 'no, I cannot,' I would not have been the candidate. When you mention candidates for public office, you are only mentioning men of affluence." *Congressional Quarterly Weekly Report*, December 5, 1969, p. 2434.

that contribute lavishly to parties and candidates are thought to be buying influence and gaining preferments of some kind in return for the money they channel into campaigns. Whether this is true may not be as important as the fact that the public, by and large, believes it to be true. In some measure, public suspicion about campaign financing contributes to public suspicion of the government itself.

Political money poses problems for the politician no less than the public. There is first the problem of raising it in large sums and second the problem of dealing with those who contribute it. In the words of a member of the U.S. Senate:

> Money? That's the dark side of the moon of politics. Nobody will really tell you all about it. I'll need $600,000 for my next campaign. You don't raise that kind of money from schoolchildren or with UNICEF drives. You look for guys who will give you five, ten, fifteen thousand, and then you remember that they did. That fellow can always get in to see you; a welfare mother can't. The real find is someone with a lot of money who doesn't want anything. They're rare, and when you find one, you guard him like your wife.[33]

Various laws have been passed by Congress and the state legislatures in attempts to curb abuses associated with financing political campaigns. At the national level their general thrust is to place restrictions on the sources of campaign money (for example, outlawing contributions from corporations and labor unions), on the size of contributions (outlawing contributions of more than $5,000 to any one federal candidate or committee), and on expenditures (a political committee may not receive or spend more than $3,000,000 in any year, candidates for the Senate cannot spend more than $10,000, and candidates for the House cannot spend more than $2,500).[34] In addition, committees and candidates are required to file financial statements with the Clerk of the House of Representatives showing their contributions and expenditures.

Critics of the laws regulating campaign finance have compiled a depressing catalogue of complaints. These laws, they find, are unworkable, unenforceable, and easily eluded. They do little to keep the lid on spending. Although national political committees cannot spend more than $3,000,000 in any year, there is no limit to the number of committees that can be formed, each one entitled to spend up to that amount. Similarly, the limitation on the amounts that candidates for Congress may spend governs only the candidates themselves; any number of individuals and groups may spend on their behalf. Big contributors can evade the restriction on the size of

---

[33] Elizabeth Drew, "Washington," *The Atlantic*, March 1971, p. 22.

[34] An alternative formula for candidates from large states and districts permits Senate candidates to spend up to a maximum of $25,000 and House candidates to spend up to a maximum of $5,000.

gifts (no more than $5,000 to any one candidate or committee) by giving to a number of candidates or committees. Although labor unions cannot siphon campaign funds from union treasuries, they are free to establish political committees (for example, COPE of the AFL-CIO) to solicit funds from members and to contribute to political campaigns. And although corporations cannot contribute directly to campaigns, there are no restrictions on giving by corporation officials except those that apply to all contributors. As for the requirement that candidates and committees must file reports on receipts and expenditures, there is scarcely anything positive to be said. The reports are often filed late and in such fragmentary form as to be of slight utility as a control over spending. Candidates can and do evade the reporting requirements with impunity, since responsibility for their enforcement is nowhere lodged. In sum, national and state laws dealing with campaign finance neither help to bring into focus nor to control the sources and uses of campaign funds. The harsh fact is that they are little more than a veneer to delude the public, and even in this respect they have met with thin success.

Reformers have not often found it easy to gain an audience of attentive legislators for the consideration of comprehensive reforms in campaign finance.[35] It seems clear that many legislators have learned to live with the existing political money system and are not anxious to see changes made in it. Numerous reforms nonetheless have been suggested. The principal recommendation considered in recent years calls for some form of tax incentive for political contributors as a means of broadening the base of campaign financing. Under the incentive plan contributors would be permitted to deduct a certain portion of their political donations on their income tax returns. In 1966, taking another tack, Congress passed the Presidential Election Campaign Fund Act, and then, on reconsideration, repealed it in 1967. Had the law remained in effect, a taxpayer would have been permitted to earmark one dollar of his taxes (on his income tax return) to finance presidential campaigns, the resulting fund to be divided equally between the two major

---

[35] A bill to limit campaign spending for political broadcasts by candidates for all federal and gubernatorial offices was passed by the 91st Congress but vetoed by President Nixon. Had the bill gone into effect, spending on political broadcasts by candidates would have been limited to 7 cents per vote (computed in terms of the preceding election) or $20,000, whichever was greater. Under this formula broadcast spending in presidential elections would be reduced by well over 50 percent. The President's veto message contended that the bill "unfairly endangers freedom of discussion, discriminates against the broadcast media, favors the incumbent officeholder over the officeseeker, and gives an unfair advantage to the famous." Moreover, he observed, the bill would plug "only one hole in a sieve." See the *Congressional Quarterly Weekly Report,* October 16, 1970, p. 2570. Critics of the President's veto saw the issue differently. The National Committee for an Effective Congress, for example, reported: "When President Nixon vetoed this measure, the first such reform in 45 years, he was obviously reflecting the self-interest of the monied party." National Committee for an Effective Congress, *Congressional Report,* January 18, 1971, p. 1.

parties. A minor party would be permitted to draw on the fund once it had received 5,000,000 votes in a presidential election. Although the law was later suspended, its passage served to recognize two important facts: first, that large amounts of money are essential for national campaigns, and second, that the public interest might be better served by widening the base of political finance and, at the same time, reducing the reliance of the parties on the "fat cats"—the large contributors.

Two other basic reforms have been suggested in recent years. One calls for a repeal of the ceilings on contributions by individuals and on expenditures by candidates and political committees. The truth of the matter is that these ceilings have proved unrealistic. Moreover, they have contributed to secret manipulations, a proliferation of committees, and evasion without penalties. In reality, the parties and candidates can spend as much as they can collect; all that is required is a little ingenuity in creating committees and in moving money in and out of them. Congruent with the proposal to eliminate ceilings is a recommendation that strict disclosure requirements be imposed concerning all aspects of political financing, followed by rigorous enforcement of the law. If candidates, parties, and contributors were required to file frequent and full disclosure statements and if the data in these reports were given wide circulation, the assumption runs, serious abuses in campaign finance would be less likely to occur. Control through publicity would supplant control through ceilings.[36]

The preeminent objectives of those who struggle to reform campaign funding are to increase public confidence in the political process, to enhance the opportunities for citizens to participate in politics by running for public office, and to reduce the vulnerability of public officials to the importunings and pressures of the big givers. The problems of political finance, in all their diversity, deserve the careful attention of the American public and its representatives. Few, if any, reforms would seem to warrant higher priority.

[36] See the recommendations of the Committee for Economic Development, *Financing a Better Election System*, pp. 20–26.

4

Political Parties
and the Electorate

It is a nagging fact of American life that for a large proportion of the population politics carries no interest, registers no significance, and excites no demands. A vast array of evidence shows the political role of the typical citizen to be that of a spectator, occasionally aroused by political events but more often inattentive to them. However tarnished this commonplace, it comes close to being the chief truth to be known about the political behavior of American citizens. Much less certain, however, is what this means. Whether it is necessary to have greatly interested and active citizens to have strong and responsible political institutions is by no means clear. No neat or simple formula exists for assessing public support for political institutions. Does the presence of a large nonvoting population reflect substantial disillusionment with the political system and its processes, or does it reflect a general satisfaction with the state of things? The answer is elusive.[1]

Whatever the consequences of low or modest turnouts for the vitality of a democratic political system, it is obvious that some American citizens use their political resources far more than others. Their political involvement is reflected not only in the fact that they vote regularly but also in the fact that they participate in politics in various other ways—perhaps by attempting to persuade other voters to support their candidates or party, by making campaign contributions, or by contributing time and energy to political campaigns. The net result of differential rates of participation is that some citizens gain access to political decision-makers and influence over their decisions, while other citizens are all but excluded from the political process.

The key to understanding the political behavior of the active American electorate is the political party. More than any other agency the party provides cues for the voters and gives shape and meaning to elections. Some voters, of course, elude party labeling, professing and preferring the role of

[1] Several studies that should be consulted on the meaning of modest rates of turnout are Walter Dean Burnham, "The Changing Shape of the American Political Universe," *American Political Science Review*, LIX (March 1965), pp. 7–28; E. E. Schattschneider, *The Semisovereign People* (New York: Holt, Rinehart and Winston, 1960), especially pp. 97–113, and Heinz Eulau, "The Politics of Happiness," *Antioch Review*, XVI (September 1956), pp. 259–264.

independent. Although their importance cannot be minimized, their consistent impact on politics falls well below that of party members. The reason
for this is partly a matter of numbers: nearly three out of four voters classify
themselves as members of one or the other of the two major parties. Before
examining the behavior of partisans and nonpartisans, however, it is appropriate to consider the broad characteristics of citizen participation in politics.

Turnout: The Diminished Electorate

There are few facts about American political behavior that stand out
more sharply than the comparatively low level of mass political involvement, as shown by voting participation. In presidential elections during the
last quarter of the nineteenth century, turnout was regularly high; in the
presidential election of 1876, for example, over 85 percent of the eligible
voters cast ballots. Beginning around the turn of the century, however, a
sharp decline in voting set in, reaching its nadir of 44 percent in 1920. A
moderate increase in turnout has taken place during the last several decades,
with participation in recent presidential elections hovering around 60 percent, still far short of the turnout levels of the last century.

Atrophy of the Electorate   Figure 5 depicts the shape of the active American
electorate over the last century. In addition to demonstrating the trends
already noted, the figure illuminates two other central voting patterns. The
first is that the decline in voting has taken place throughout the nation, albeit
more markedly in the South. The second is that voting participation in the
United States falls noticeably below that of other nations in the Western
World, where turnout in national elections consistently ranges between 80
and 95 percent. Although these data on American voting participation are
far from complimentary, they may conceal more of the problem than they
uncover. The hard truth is that turnout is even less impressive in nonpresidential elections. In the off-year elections of the 1950s, for example, only
slightly over 40 percent of the eligible voters cast ballots for members of
Congress. In the two off-year congressional elections of the 1960s (1962 and
1966), the turnout percentages were only 47 and 46, respectively. Many state
and local elections fail to achieve even these modest levels of participation. It
remains to be observed that the low point in participation is ordinarily
plumbed in primary elections—a total primary vote of 20 to 25 percent of
the potential electorate is not uncommon. In the one-party Democratic states
of the South, however, participation in primary elections is consistently much

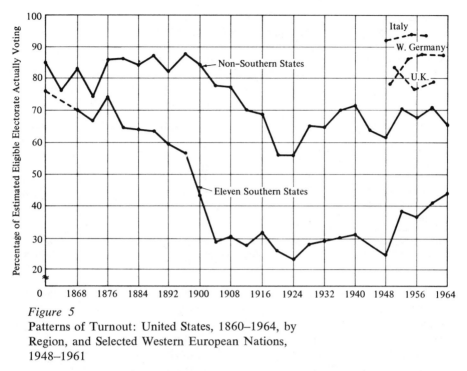

Figure 5

Patterns of Turnout: United States, 1860–1964, by
Region, and Selected Western European Nations,
1948–1961

Source: Walter Dean Burnham, "The Changing Shape of the American Political Universe,"
American Political Science Review, LIX (March 1965), p. 11.

higher than in general elections.[2] (See Table 10). In sum, it is a large and
uncomfortable fact of American political life that a great many citizens—
comprising at least one-third of the eligible electorate even in presidential
years—are almost wholly detached from the political system and the processes through which its leaders are selected.

There are a number of reasons for the poor performance of twentieth-
century American electorates. In the case of the southern states it is plain
that the limitations placed on Negro suffrage shortly before the turn of the
century drastically curtailed their participation. A variety of legal abridge-
ments and strategies, buttressed by social and economic sanctions of all
kinds, effectively disfranchised all but the most persistent and resourceful
black citizens. The ingenuity of southern white politicians during this era can
scarcely be exaggerated. Poll taxes, literacy tests, understanding-the-

[2] The explanation for this is well known: often the only significant choice among
candidates available to southern voters is to be found in Democratic primaries. As the
Republican party gains competitive strength in the South, participation in general elections is virtually certain to increase.

Table 10

Mean Voting Turnout in Primary and General Elections
For Governor and U.S. Senator, 1956–1960*

	PERCENT VOTING FOR GOVERNOR			PERCENT VOTING FOR U.S. SENATOR		
State Groups	*Prim. Elect.*	*Gen. Elect.*	*Difference*	*Prim. Elect.*	*Gen. Elect.*	*Difference*
One-Party Democratic	32.5%	17.0%	+15.5%	22.8%	19.2%	+ 3.6%
Modified One-Party Democratic	28.5	41.3	−12.8	25.7	40.7	−15.0
Two-Party	25.4	59.2	−33.8	21.5	58.3	−36.8
Modified One-Party Republican	21.9	56.9	−35.0	22.7	55.3	−32.6

Source: Austin Ranney, "Parties in State Politics," in Herbert Jacob and Kenneth N. Vines, (eds.), *Politics in the American States*, p. 75. Copyright © 1965, Little, Brown and Company, Inc. Reprinted by permission.

constitution tests, white primaries,[3] stringent residence and registration requirements, and discriminatory registration administration—all were consciously employed by dominant elites to maintain a white electorate and thus to settle political questions within the white community.

Another prime reason for the sharp contraction of the active electorate stems from the advent of one-party politics throughout large sections of the country. Democratic domination of the South began shortly after the Civil War Reconstruction governments were terminated. Nevertheless, even in the 1880s, the Republican presidential vote was at least half of the Democratic vote in all but a few southern states. The election of 1896, one of the most decisive elections in American history, culminated in the virtual disappearance of the Republican party in the South and in a precipitate drop in Democratic strength in the North. E. E. Schattschneider's analysis of this election is instructive:

> The 1896 party cleavage resulted from the tremendous reaction of conservatives in both major parties to the Populist movement, a radical agrarian agitation that alarmed people of substance all over the country. . . . Southern

[3] The white primary in southern states resulted from the exclusion of Negroes from membership in the Democratic party, which was held to be a "private" organization. Since the real election at this time in most southern states occurred in the Democratic primaries, there was little opportunity for Negroes to make their influence felt. After many years of litigation, the Supreme Court in 1944 held that the white primary was in violation of the Fifteenth Amendment. The Court's position in *Smith* vs *Allwright* was that the primary is an integral part of the election process and that political parties are engaged in a public rather than a private function in holding primary elections. After the white primary was held unconstitutional, southern states turned to the development of literacy and understanding tests, along with discriminatory registration systems, in order to bar Negro access to the polls.

conservatives reacted so strongly that they were willing to revive the tensions and animosities of the Civil War and the Reconstruction in order to set up a one-party sectional southern political monopoly in which nearly all Negroes and many poor whites were disfranchised. . . . The northern conservatives were so badly frightened by the Bryan candidacy that they adopted drastic measures to alarm the country. As a matter of fact, the conservative reaction to Bryanism in the North was almost as spectacular as the conservative reaction to Populism in the South. As a result the Democratic party in large areas of the Northeast and Middle West was wiped out, or decimated, while the Republican party consolidated its supremacy in all of the most populous areas of the country. The resulting party lineup was one of the most sharply sectional political divisions in American history. . . . Both sections became more conservative because *one-party politics tends strongly to vest political power in the hands of the people who already have enormous power.* Moreover, in one-party areas (areas of extreme sectionalism) votes decline in value because the voters no longer have a valuable party alternative.[4]

The smothering effect of a noncompetitive environment on participation can be seen in election turnouts following the realignment of the 1890s. Consider this evidence: between 1884 and 1904 turnout in Virginia dropped 57 percent, in Mississippi, 51 percent, and in Louisiana, 50 percent. Part of the explanation for these drop-offs undoubtedly can be associated with the success of southern efforts to disfranchise Negroes, but it is also clear that one-party politics had a decisive impact on the electorate. In the first place, the drop in participation was too large to be accounted for merely by the disappearance of black votes. Second, the impact of the new sectionalism was not confined simply to the South. Despite their growing populations, some fourteen northern states had smaller turnouts in 1904 than they did in 1896.[5] What emerges from these findings is that one-party politics depresses political participation because it robs the electorate of choice. Not surprisingly, interest atrophies. Whether one votes or not may become a matter of slight moment.[6]

[4] From *The Semisovereign People* by E. E. Schattschneider. Copyright © 1960 by E. E. Schattschneider. Reprinted by permission of Holt, Rinehart and Winston, Inc., pp. 78–80.

[5] Schattschneider, *The Semisovereign People*, p. 84.

[6] A number of recent studies have found a significant relationship between the degree of competitiveness between the parties and the presence of high levels of participation. Put simply, the proposition is that the more competitive the party environment, the greater the probability that turnout levels will be high. This finding holds for both southern and northern states. See Richard E. Dawson and James A. Robinson, "Inter-Party Competition, Economic Variables, and Welfare Policies in the American States," *Journal of Politics*, XXV (May 1963), pp. 265–289; Lester W. Milbrath, "Political Participation in the States," in Herbert Jacob and Kenneth N. Vines (eds.), *Politics in the American States* (Boston: Little, Brown, 1965), p. 43. Another study discloses that registration rates are higher in cities located in competitive states than in those located in noncompetitive states. Stanley Kelley, Jr., *et al.*, "Registration and Voting: Putting First Things First," *American Political Science Review*, LXI (June 1967), pp. 363–366.

Still other reasons have been advanced for the decline in mass political involvement in this century. One concerns woman suffrage. Although women were given the vote in 1920, it is obvious that large numbers of them were indifferent to their new right and did not use it immediately. In subsequent decades a significantly larger proportion of women entered the active electorate, though even today their participation rate falls well below that of men.[7] In similar vein, it is argued that the level of participation was lowered as a result of the large numbers of immigrants who entered the country around the turn of the century but who were slow to become involved in the nation's political life. Indeed, it seems likely that a partial explanation for the upswing in participation beginning in the late 1920s was that both women and foreign-stock populations moved into the active electorate in greater numbers.

The argument has often been made, both in scholarly studies and popular accounts, that failure to vote is in large measure attributable to socioeconomic forces—that is, that nonvoters stay away from the polls because they are unconcerned over elections and are unable to perceive any personal stakes in election outcomes. There is, of course, a good case to be made for this view.[8] Nevertheless, it tells something less than the whole story and may unduly diminish the significance of political forces in explaining nonparticipation. Recent research by Stanley Kelley, Jr. on the impact of registration laws on turnout in 104 of the nation's largest cities helps to place political explanations for nonparticipation in perspective. Several findings in this study are especially important. A strong correlation was found between the existence of literacy test provisions and lower registration rates; that is, those cities located in states with literacy tests had a lower proportion of the voting-age population registered to vote. Another strong relationship was found between the date for closing registration rolls and the proportion of

---

[7] One careful estimate is that voting participation among women is about 10 percent below that of men. Although college-educated women turn out for elections at about the same rate as college-educated men, poorly educated women vote less frequently than men with similar education. See Angus Campbell, Philip E. Converse, Warren E. Miller, and Donald E. Stokes, *The American Voter* (New York: Wiley, 1960), pp. 484–485.

[8] One thrust in this interpretation is represented in the writings of E. E. Schattschneider: "It is profoundly characteristic of the behavior of the more fortunate strata of the community that responsibility for widespread nonparticipation is attributed wholly to the ignorance, indifference, and shiftlessness of the people. This has always been the rationalization used to justify the exclusion of the lower classes from any political system. There is a better explanation. Abstention reflects the suppression of the options and alternatives that reflect the needs of the nonparticipants. . . . It has been assumed that only legal barriers inhibited the disfranchised. We know better now. The exclusion of people by extralegal processes, by social processes, by the way the political system is organized and structured may be far more effective than the law." From *The Semisovereign People* by E. E. Schattschneider. Copyright © 1960 by E. E. Schattschneider. Reprinted by permission of Holt, Rinehart and Winston, pp. 104–105, 111.

the voting-age population that was registered. By moving the closing date for registration from one month to one week before the election, the study suggests, it would be possible to increase registration by nearly four percent. Most important, there is evidence that differences among cities in turnout are significantly related to differences in rates of registration, which in turn reflect differences in the ease with which citizens may register to vote. The absence of literacy tests, a late closing date for registration, the presence of permanent (rather than periodic) registration—all are associated with higher turnout at the polls. Of special interest in this study was the finding that in those American cities in which more than 90 percent of the voting-age population were registered to vote, the turnout of voters exceeded the average turnouts in postwar national elections in Canada, France, and Great Britain, each of which employs a system of automatic registration.[9]

From the standpoint of turnout, it seems clear that stringent registration rules have had a pernicious effect. During the latter part of the nineteenth century when turnout was regularly between 75 and 85 percent of the eligible electorate, there were many parts of the country where voters were not required to register or where automatic registration was in effect. During the period from 1896 to 1924, when turnout dropped steadily, a great many states adopted registration laws that required prospective voters to register annually in person. The effect of these laws undoubtedly was to keep many citizens away from the polls. Since 1924 turnout has gradually increased; significantly, this has occurred at a time when many states have liberalized their rules governing registration. "Turnout in presidential elections in the United States may have declined and then risen again," Kelley writes, "not because of changes in the *interest* of voters in elections, but because of changes in the *interest demanded* of them."[10]

Expansion of the Electorate   The argument of these pages is that the decline in the size of the active American electorate has been due to a number of factors. Restrictions on black voting, the introduction of women and foreign-born into the voting population, the spread of one-party politics, and the development of cumbersome and restrictive registration systems—all have contributed in some measure to the constriction of the electorate in the twentieth century. In the last several decades, however, a gradual increase in voting participation has occurred. Passage of the Voting Rights Act of 1965—the main thrusts of which were to suspend literacy tests and other voter qualification devices in any state or county in which less than 50 percent of the voting-age residents were registered to vote on November 1, 1964, and to authorize the appointment of federal voting examiners to assist persons

[9] Kelley, "Registration and Voting," pp. 359–379.
[10] Kelley, "Registration and Voting," p. 374.

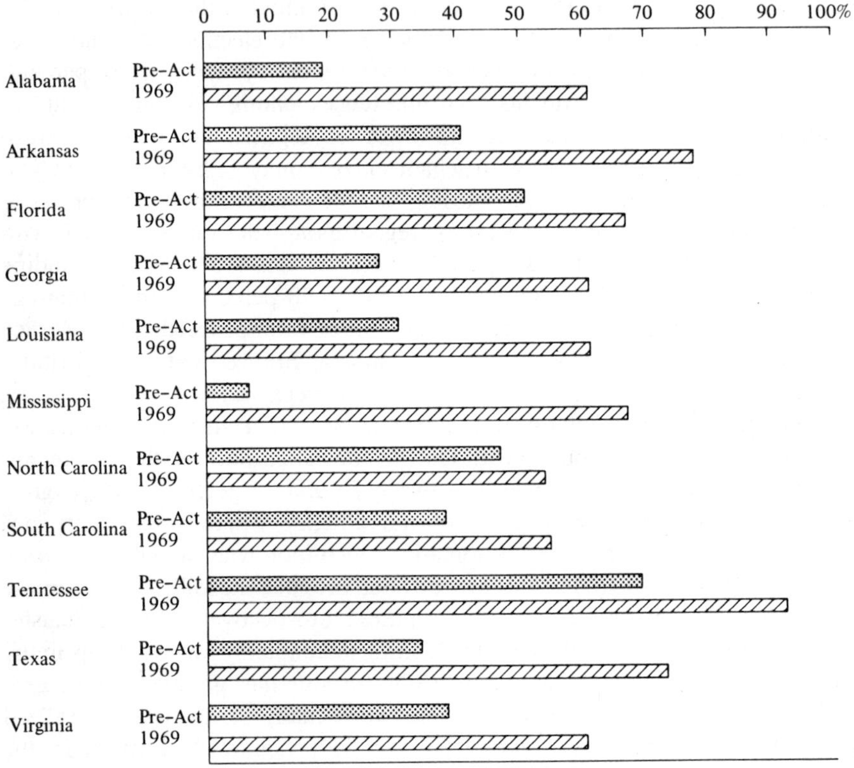

Figure 6
Percentage of Voting Age Negro Population
Registered to Vote, Prior to Voting Rights Act of 1965
and in 1969, Eleven Southern States

Source: Pre-act registration data appear in a report of the United States Commission on Civil Rights, *Political Participation* (Washington, D.C.: Government Printing Office, 1968), pp. 222–223; 1969 data furnished by the Voter Education Project of the Southern Regional Council. For most of the states, the pre-act registration figures are those of 1964; the Texas data are for 1961.

who meet state requirements to register—has had a dramatic impact on black political participation in the South. (See Figure 6). Assuming that further expansion of the active electorate is desirable, what steps might be taken to bring this about?

There are a number of traditional restraints on voting that clearly have had a deleterious impact on participation, serving either to deprive citizens of the right to vote or to impose such heavy costs on them in time and effort as to discourage their voting. The Commission on Registration and Voting Participation established by President Kennedy in 1963 offered a variety of recommendations designed to eliminate these obstacles.[11] Unwieldy and complicated registration systems were seen by the Commission as one of the principal restraints on widespread participation. Among other things, the report recommended that states liberalize their registration laws by providing for door-to-door canvassing by registrars to compile registers of voters,[12] precinct and mobile registration, permanent and personal registration under which no citizen's registration would be cancelled for failure to vote in any period of less than four years, a late closing date for registration, and absentee registration. In addition, the Commission recommended that the states consider prohibition of the uses of registration lists for any purposes other than electoral.[13] A miscellany of recommendations by the Commission include the call for making elections legal holidays, liberalization of absentee voting provisions, late closing of the polls, and, where necessary, an increase in the number of polling places.

One of the Commission's major recommendations for easing residency requirements was met by the 91st Congress through the adoption of amendments to the Voting Rights Act of 1965.[14] In addition to lowering the voting age from 21 to 18 for all federal, state, and local elections and suspending literacy tests for five years, all residency requirements of more than 30 days for voting in federal elections were eliminated. In late 1970 the Supreme Court upheld parts of this legislation, including the provisions concerning residency requirements and the suspension of literacy tests. Significantly, although validating the right of 18-year-olds to vote in federal elections, the

[11] *Report on Registration and Voting Participation* (Washington, D.C.: U.S. Government Printing Office, 1963).

[12] Many countries employ a system of automatic registration that requires municipal officials, rather than individual voters, to take the initiative for registration. These officials regularly compile lists of electors, incorporating the names of those citizens newly eligible to vote. The registration law of Canada requires local officials to visit each home to register eligible voters. The state of Idaho has a similar law, and turnout there is very high, occasionally over 80 percent. *Report on Registration and Voting Participation*, p. 32.

[13] There is some evidence that persons decide not to register in those states which permit local officials to use registration lists for tax assessment, jury selection, and other extraneous public purposes.

[14] According to a survey by the Bureau of the Census in 1968, nearly 27 million people of voting age were not registered to vote. About 10 percent of this number reported they were not registered because they were "not a citizen." Another 11 percent cited their failure to satisfy residence requirements. About 13 percent reported they were unable to register because of lack of transportation, illness, or work demands. A whopping 53 percent stated that they were not interested in the election or in politics in general or expressed dislike for the political process. Miscellaneous reasons accounted for the remainder of the sample. Among nonregistered persons with five or more years of college, 33 percent reported inability to meet residence requirements as the reason for nonregistration. Only 2 percent of those persons who had completed less than five years of elementary school cited this reason. U.S. Bureau of the Census, "Voting and Registration in the Election of November 1968," *Current Population Reports* (Washington, D.C.: U.S. Government Printing Office, 1969), p. 4.

Court held that Congress had exceeded its constitutional powers in authorizing 18-year-old voting in state and local elections. With the adoption of the 26th Amendment to the Constitution in mid-1971, the voting age for all elections was lowered to 18.

No country in the world has as complex a system of registration and voting as the United States. Without doubt, these arrangements have diminished the possibilities for electoral frauds and have helped to sustain public confidence in the election process. But a heavy price has been paid for these controls. The blunt truth of the matter is that rigid and cumbersome arrangements have inhibited voter participation. There is good reason to believe that restrictions could be eased substantially without sacrificing the necessary checks that preserve the integrity of the ballot. The result very likely would be a significantly expanded active electorate.

Forms of Political Participation

There are numerous forms of political participation open to the American people, as shown by Table 11. Several conclusions may be derived from this portrait of America's participatory habits in politics. An initial reaction to the data is likely to be that individuals diverge widely in the ways they respond to opportunities for participation in politics. On closer inspection, however, there is less divergence than might be supposed. Some forms of participation, such as expressing one's views on political matters, exact from the individual a small cost in time and effort; indeed, though an overwhelming proportion of the electorate admits to a willingness to express political views when asked, less than half (possibly far less than half), are likely to hold informed opinions. Other forms of participation, such as involvement in campaigns or attendance at political meetings, require a substantially greater commitment on the part of the citizen. What seems clear beyond doubt is that very few Americans lie awake nights pondering how they can become immediately involved in influencing political events and the course of politics. They participate mainly through voicing opinions—and perhaps attempting to influence others—and through voting. Perhaps 3 to 10 percent of the people will attend political meetings, contribute money to political campaigns, join a political club or organization, or provide some form of leadership in campaigns. It may not be overly harsh to suggest that, apart from voting, the participation of most Americans in politics has no more lasting impact than a stone cast in the water. At the least, the active participation of the typical American comes close to the point of irreducible minimum.

Table 11
A Profile of American Political Participation*

Mode of Political Participation	Estimated Proportion of Americans as Participants
Opinion Participation:	
Normally express political opinions when asked	70–90%
Normally express informed political opinions when asked	30–50
Possess basic "textbook" information of politics	15–40
Leadership Participation:	
Personal leadership (attempts to influence political views of others through discussion)	50–70
Voluntary leadership in political campaigns	3–5
Partisan precinct leadership	.25–1
Voter Participation:	
Infrequent participants (vote occasionally in elections)	30–40
Regular participants (vote consistently in all elections)— national, state, and local)	25–30
Apoliticals (voting in no elections)	3–7
Partisan Participation:	
Party identifiers (consider themselves as Republicans or Democrats)	65–75
Attend political meetings, rallies, dinners, and so on	5–7
Support financially campaigns of parties or candidates	4–10
Actual membership in a political club or organization	2–3
Voluntary Organized Participation:	
Membership in organization of any kind	60–65
Membership in organizations that sometimes take stands on political issues	30–35

* Source: Dan Nimmo and Thomas D. Ungs, *American Political Patterns: Conflict and Consensus*, p. 135. Copyright © 1967 by Little, Brown and Company, Inc. Reprinted by permission.

Cumulative Involvement in Politics   The evidence from a number of studies of political participation is that people do not participate randomly in politics. Rather, there is a hierarchy of political involvement, as suggested in Figure 7, drawn from a study by Lester W. Milbrath.[15] Individuals who are actively involved in politics engage in a wide variety of political acts. The outstanding characteristic of their participation is that it is cumulative. The active members of a political party, for example, are likely to be found soliciting political funds, contributing time and money to campaigns, attending meetings, and so on. Individuals who are minimally involved in politics engage only in such limited activities as those grouped near the base

[15] Lester W. Milbrath, *Political Participation* (Chicago: Rand McNally, 1965), pp. 17–21.

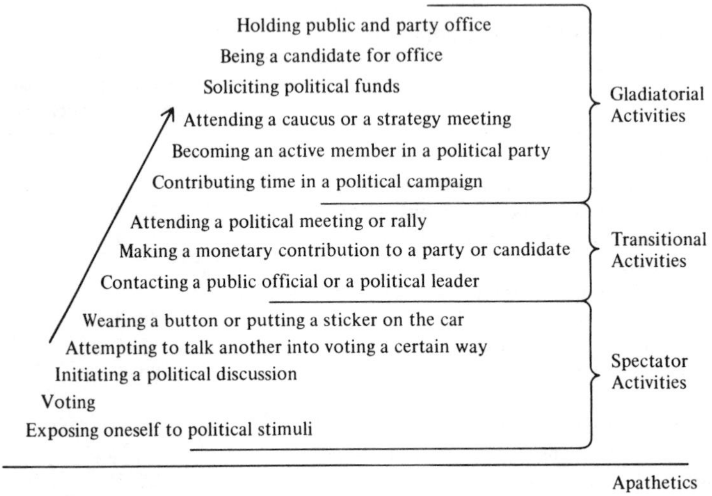

Holding public and party office
Being a candidate for office
Soliciting political funds
Attending a caucus or a strategy meeting
Becoming an active member in a political party
Contributing time in a political campaign

Gladiatorial
Activities

Attending a political meeting or rally
Making a monetary contribution to a party or candidate
Contacting a public official or a political leader

Transitional
Activities

Wearing a button or putting a sticker on the car
Attempting to talk another into voting a certain way
Initiating a political discussion
Voting
Exposing oneself to political stimuli

Spectator
Activities

Apathetics

Figure 7
Hierarchy of Political Involvement

Source: Lester W. Milbrath, *Political Participation* (Chicago: Rand McNally & Company, 1965), p. 18.

of the hierarchy. At the very bottom are those persons who stand on the out-skirts of the political world, scarcely, if at all, aware of the political forces that play upon them or of the opportunities open to them to use their resources (including the vote) to gain political objectives.

Some portion of the explanation for the passivity of American citizens may lie with the parties themselves. There is little evidence that the parties are active in clearing the road for popular participation. A recent survey discloses that only a small proportion of citizens are contacted (either called upon personally or telephoned) by party workers in an effort to get them to vote for the candidates of their party. Immediately prior to the 1968 presidential election, for example, only 8 percent of a national sample reported that they had been contacted by Democratic party workers, and only 12 percent were contacted by Republican workers. The individuals most likely to come into contact with the electioneering activities of the parties are those with high socioeconomic status—in particular those with a college education, a professional or business background, and a high income.[16] For most Americans the party organization, *qua* organization, is all but invisible. The

[16] *Gallup Opinion Index, Report No. 41*, November 1968, pp. 2–3. A variety of studies have shown that personal contact by a party worker is one of the principal stimulants to political participation. It not only increases the probability that the person contacted will vote but also that he will undertake certain activities on behalf of the party. See Milbrath, *Political Participation*, pp. 99–101.

"That's the trouble with a *truly* enlightened electorate."

Drawing by D. Fradon; © 1968 The New Yorker Magazine, Inc.

passivity of the ordinary citizen is almost matched by the passivity of the party organizations.

The Active and Passive Citizenry   A number of social, demographic, and political variables are related to the act of voting. Table 12 provides a profile of those citizens who are more likely to turn out at elections and

Table 12
A Profile of the More Active and
Less Active Citizenry*

More Likely to Vote	*Less Likely to Vote*
High income	Low income
High occupational status	Low occupational status
College education	Grade school education
Male	Female
Middle-aged	Young or old
Urban resident	Rural resident
Metropolitan area resident	Small town resident
White	Negro
Northern state resident	Southern state resident
Resident in competitive party environment	Resident in noncompetitive party environment
Union member	Nonunion labor
Homeowner	Renter
Jews and Catholics	Protestants

* These findings result from a large number of studies of the American electorate. For a summary and analysis of this literature, see Lester W. Milbrath, *Political Participation* (Chicago: Rand McNally, 1965).

those who are less likely to turn out. Some of the factors, it will be seen, are closely related—for example, high income, high occupational status, and college education. For all their interest the distinctions drawn in the table cannot be taken wholly at face value. The lower turnout of Protestants, for example, is undoubtedly due in part to the lower levels of participation of southern and of rural voters, who happen to be largely Protestant. Moreover, not all the variables carry equal significance. By all odds the best social indicators of voting participation are those that reflect socioeconomic status: income, occupation, and education.

Citizens who show enthusiasm for voting and who participate regularly in elections can be distinguished by their psychological makeup as well as by their social and economic backgrounds. The prospect that a person will vote is heavily influenced by the intensity of his partisan preference: the more substantial his commitment to a party, the stronger the probability that he will vote.[17] The person who has a strong partisan preference and who perceives the election as likely to be close is virtually certain to vote. The voter can also be distinguished by other indices of psychological involvement

Table 13
Relation of Sense of Political Efficacy to
Voting Turnout, 1956*

| | SENSE OF POLITICAL EFFICACY | | | | |
	Low				*High*
Voted	52%	60%	75%	84%	91%
Did not vote	48	40	25	16	9
	100	100	100	100	100
Number of cases	263	343	461	501	196

Source: Angus Campbell, Philip E. Converse, Warren E. Miller, and Donald E. Stokes, *The American Voter* (New York: John Wiley and Sons, 1960), p. 105.

[17] The *popular* view has often held that independents are more likely than partisans to be intelligently and actively involved in political affairs. At least until the middle 1960s, survey-research data showed scant support for this portrait of the independent. Rather, the independent emerged as a person who was less attentive to politics, less informed on issues, and less concerned over election outcomes than partisans. For this view, see Campbell *et al.*, *The American Voter*, p. 143. A recent study suggests, however, that the sharp increase of late in the number of independents among voters with college educations, higher incomes, and white-collar occupations may mean that there are ". . . at least *two* groups of independents: 'old independents' who correspond to the rather bleak classical survey-research picture, and 'new independents' who may have declined to identify with either major party not because they are relatively politically unconscious, but because the structure of electoral politics at the present time turns upon parties, issues, and symbolisms which do not have much meaning in terms of their political values or cognitions." See Walter Dean Burnham, *Critical Elections and the Mainsprings of American Politics* (New York: Norton, 1970), p. 127.

in political affairs. Survey research data show him to be highly interested in campaigns and concerned over election outcomes. He is much more likely than the nonvoter to possess a strong sense of political efficacy—that is, a disposition to see his own participation in politics as important and effective. (See Table 13). Finally, in sharp contrast to the nonvoter, the voter accepts the norm that voting is a civic obligation, a responsibility not to be taken lightly. In sum, the evidence is plain that psychological involvement— marked by interest in elections, concern over their outcome, a sense of political efficacy, and a sense of citizen duty—is a major explanation for participation in elections.[18]

Party Identification in the Electorate

Table 14 reveals one of the firm landmarks of American politics: the large number of voters (approximately 75 percent) who consider themselves to be adherents of one or the other of the two major parties. Over the last two decades there has been surprisingly little change in the distribution of party identification in the electorate, except for the growth in the number of independents. In the typical survey during this period, between 45 and 50 percent of the respondents have identified themselves as Democrats, with the remainder about evenly divided between Republicans and independents. In 1964, a high point of Democratic advantage, Democratic identifiers outnumbered Republican identifiers by a margin of over two-to-one. Under the circumstances the magnitude of Lyndon Johnson's victory over Barry Goldwater—winning by a margin in excess of 15 million votes—cannot be seen as altogether astonishing.

Table 14
The Distribution of Party Identification in the
Electorate, 1940–1970*

	1940	1950	1952	1954	1956	1958	1960	1962	1964	1966	1968	1970
Democrat	42	45	47	47	44	47	46	47	53	48	46	44
Republican	38	33	27	27	29	29	27	27	25	27	27	29
Independent	20	22	22	22	24	19	23	23	22	25	27	27
Apolitical (don't know)			4	4	3	5	4	3				

* Sources: For the years 1940, 1950, 1964–1970, the data source is the *Gallup Opinion Index, Report No. 38* and *62* (Princeton, N.J.: 1968, 1970); for the years 1952–1962, the source is the Survey Research Center of the University of Michigan, as reported in Angus Campbell *et al., Elections and the Political Order* (New York: John Wiley and Sons, Inc., 1966), p. 13.

[18] Campbell *et al., The American Voter*, pp. 101–107.

The Significance of Party Identification   When the distribution of underlying loyalties in the electorate is understood, there is less mystery as to the Democratic party's successes in national elections in recent decades. The Democratic party launches each campaign with nearly two out of every three partisans affiliated in one degree or another with its candidates. If it can assemble the support of most of those who identify themselves as Democrats and make a reasonable showing among independents, it is certain to win. By contrast, the task of the Republican party is much more formidable. Not only must it retain and mobilize its own partisans, but it must also carry a major share of the independents and attract a significant number of Democratic partisans as well. Republican prospects would be thin at best were it not for the fact that the turnout rate of Democratic partisans is much lower than that of Republicans.[19] The effect of this lower level of participation, one study suggests, is to reduce the normal Democratic proportion of the two-party popular vote to about 53 or 54 percent.[20]

The distribution of party followings in the electorate places the Republican party at a substantial disadvantage. It can win national elections only if it offers candidates or issues of sufficient appeal to offset the normal Democratic majority. Consider several recent examples of Republican success. The 1952 Republican victory appears to have resulted from the convergence of three factors: disenchantment with the Truman Administration, the personal magnetism of Eisenhower, and widespread public frustration over the Korean war. Four years later the Republican majority was due principally to candidate appeal—to the public's high regard for President Eisenhower as a person.[21] In the 1956 election Eisenhower lost the votes of only a small fraction of Republican identifiers and received the support of about three out of four independents and about one out of four Democrats.[22] Despite the exceptional appeal of Eisenhower, the underlying support for the Democratic party was sufficient to permit it to capture both houses of Congress.

"Short term" forces again were of critical importance in the victory of Richard M. Nixon in the 1968 presidential election. Although the underlying distribution of party loyalties remained about the same as in 1964, a "sense of cumulative grievance" with the Johnson Administration led many Democrats to abandon their party. The disillusionment of voters over the Adminis-

---

[19] A disposition to participate in elections is related to high interest, information, and involvement. The Democratic vote regularly suffers from the fact that citizens who might be expected to vote Democratic—those in the lower socioeconomic strata—are often not sufficiently interested or involved in the election to turn out on election day.

[20] Philip E. Converse, Angus Campbell, Warren E. Miller, and Donald E. Stokes, "Stability and Change in 1960: A Reinstating Election," *American Political Science Review*, LV (June 1961), p. 274.

[21] Campbell *et al., The American Voter*, pp. 525–527.

[22] Angus Campbell, "A Classification of the Presidential Elections," in *Elections and the Political Order* (New York: Wiley, 1966), p. 72.

tration's handling of the Vietnam war, the racial crisis, and the "law and order" issue was so great that a full 30 percent of all white voters (both Democrats and Republicans) who supported Lyndon Johnson in 1964 switched to Richard Nixon or George Wallace in 1968 (with Nixon the beneficiary by a 4-to-1 ratio). Very probably the polarization of the races has never been greater than in 1968, when nearly 90 percent of the black voters voted for the Democratic nominee, Hubert Humphrey, as contrasted with less than 35 percent of the white voters. Despite the substantial shift of Democratic identifiers to Nixon or Wallace in the presidential race, there was little change at other levels of government. The Republican party gained only four seats in the U.S. House of Representatives and only five seats in the Senate. At the state legislative level the Democratic proportion of seats declined hardly at all—from 57.7 percent of the seats to 57.5 percent. Democratic dominance in the electorate thus remained firm at all but the presidential level.[23]

The most significant features of the party identification of the electorate are the high proportion of citizens who identify with either the Democratic or the Republican party and the persistence of their loyalties. About two out of three Americans hold the same party attachment as their parents. Moreover, in presidential elections, a majority of people testify that they have always supported the candidate of their party.[24] Without doubt party affiliation is the single most important variable in explaining voting behavior. Nonetheless, there are many voters who steadily spurn the claims of party. Increasingly, these independents have been at the decisive center of American elections, holding the balance of power between the major parties. Over one-quarter of the national electorate can be categorized in terms of its independence from the parties. This large bloc of voters is not only a prime target of the parties but also volatile in its behavior. A glance at Table 15 will reveal that independents voted strongly Democratic in the 1940s, strongly Republican in the 1950s, and alternated between the parties in the 1960s. In all elections over this period except 1960, a majority of the independents supported the winning presidential candidate, always by a margin in excess of his national average.

Party Identification and Presidential Elections   Presidential elections can be classified in broad contour by examining the relationship between election outcomes and the pattern of party loyalties present in the electorate. Three basic types of elections can be identified: maintaining, deviating, and realign-

---

[23] Philip E. Converse, Warren E. Miller, Jerrold G. Rusk, and Arthur G. Wolfe, "Continuity and Change in American Politics: Parties and Issues in the 1968 Election," *American Political Science Review,* LXIII (December 1969), pp. 1083–1105.
[24] Campbell *et al., The American Voter,* p. 148.

Table 15
The Distribution of Votes for President by
Independents, 1940–1968*

	1940	1944	1948	1952	1956	1960	1964	1968
Democratic	61%	62%	57%	33%	27%	46%	66%	27%
Republican	39	38	43	67	73	54	34	56
American Independent								17
Total	100	100	100	100	100	100	100	100
$n =$				263	309	298	219	286
		(Gallup Poll)			(Survey Research Center)			

* Source: William H. Flanigan, *Political Behavior of the American Electorate* (Boston: Allyn and Bacon, Inc., 1968), p. 40. (Data covering 1940–1964 from Flanigan; 1968 data from Survey Research Center.)

ing.[25] A "maintaining" election is described as one in which the pattern of party attachments in the electorate fixes the outcome; the winning party owes its victory to the fact that more voters identify with it than with any other party. A "deviating" election, by contrast, is one in which existing party loyalties are temporarily displaced by short-term forces, enabling the minority (or second) party to win the presidency. In a "realigning" election the majority party in the electorate not only loses the election but also finds that many of its previous supporters have abandoned their loyalties and moved into the ranks of the other party. So fundamental is the transformation of partisan attachments that the second party becomes the majority party.

The most common form of presidential election is that in which the party dominant in the electorate wins the presidency—that is, a maintaining election. Most of the Republican victories during the last half of the nineteenth century and the first quarter of the twentieth century would be classified as maintaining elections. Recent elections of this type occurred in 1948, 1960, and 1964—all elections won by the Democratic party. The dynamics of a maintaining election are furnished by the majority party; the minority party loses because it has been unable to develop either issues or candidates sufficiently attractive to upset the prevailing pattern of party affiliation.

It is not surprising that on occasion party loyalties fail to hold and that the party that occupies minority status in terms of electoral preferences wins the presidential office. Although the Republicans clearly held an electoral majority in the early twentieth century, Woodrow Wilson was twice elected President—in 1912, when the Republican party was split between Roosevelt and Taft, and in 1916, when his incumbency and the war issue were sufficient to give him a slight edge. More recent examples are the elections of 1952, 1956, and 1968. Both victories of Dwight D. Eisenhower in the 1950s were

[25] These categories are drawn from Campbell, *et al.*, *The American Voter*, pp. 531–538.

achieved in the face of heavy Democratic majorities in the electorate. Richard Nixon's narrow victory in 1968 came at a time when two out of every three partisans were identified with the Democratic party. Taken as a group, deviating elections tend to be characterized by dramatic issues, charismatic personalities, or sharp factional conflict within the majority party. Ticket splitting becomes the order of the day. Despite the appeal of the minority party's presidential candidate, his coattails have rarely been strong enough to give his party control of Congress. Hence, deviating elections are likely to result in one party controlling the presidency and the other party controlling the Congress.

The familiar terrain of American politics is sharply changed as a result of realigning elections. These elections are episodic and drastic. Large numbers of voters move out of the majority party and into the minority party, switching not only their vote at that election but also their long-term party allegiance. The most recent examples of realigning elections are those of 1896 and 1932. In the case of the former, a great many Democrats left their party following the financial panic of 1893, voted for McKinley in 1896, and became part of the strong Republican majority that dominated the country until 1932. An even sharper upheaval in the electorate occurred in the election of 1932, when the normal Republican majority collapsed as a result of the Great Depression. Franklin D. Roosevelt was swept into office, and millions of Republicans shifted, more or less permanently, into the ranks of the Democratic party. The realignment of the parties brought about in 1932 remains largely intact today. Realigning elections are the products of major crises, of disturbances so severe that not even traditional party loyalties can survive.

The Voting Behavior of Social Groups

The role of social groups should not be overlooked in unraveling the behavior of the American electorate. It has long been known that the voting behavior of individuals is influenced not only by their personal values and predilections (often derived from family party attachment) but also by their affiliations with social groups.[26] Table 16 indicates the relationships between

---

[26] Studies of electoral behavior that bear too heavily on the group as the unit of analysis may do some injustice to the individual voter, making him appear as an object to be managed by skillful propagandists or as the victim of social determinants (for example, his occupation, race, or education). Preoccupation with the gross characteristics of voters may lead the analyst to minimize the individual's awareness and concern over issues. V. O. Key, Jr., has argued that ". . . the electorate behaves about as rationally and responsibly as we should expect, given the clarity of the alternatives presented to it and the character of the information available to it." By and large, in Key's study, the American voter emerges as a rational and responsible person concerned over matters of public policy, governmental performance, and executive personality. See V. O. Key, Jr. (with Milton C. Cummings), *The Responsible Electorate* (New York: Vintage Books, 1966), p. 7.

Table 16
Vote by Groups in Presidential Elections, 1952–1968*

| | 1952 | | 1956 | | 1960 | | 1964 | | 1968 | | *Wallace* |
	Dem.	*Rep.*	*Dem.*	*Rep.*	*Dem.*	*Rep.*	*Dem.*	*Rep.*	*Dem.*	*Rep.*	
	%	%	%	%	%	%	%	%	%	%	%
National	4.6	55.4	42.2	57.8	50.1	49.9	61.3	38.7	43.0	43.4	13.6
Men	47	53	45	55	52	48	60	40	41	43	16
Women	42	58	39	61	49	51	62	38	45	43	12
White	43	57	41	59	49	51	59	41	38	47	15
Nonwhite	79	21	61	39	68	32	94	6	85	12	3
College	34	66	31	69	39	61	52	48	37	54	9
High School	45	55	42	58	52	48	62	38	42	43	15
Grade School	52	48	50	50	55	45	66	34	52	33	15
Professional and Business	36	64	32	68	42	58	54	46	34	56	10
White Collar	40	60	37	63	48	52	57	43	41	47	12
Manual	55	45	50	50	60	40	71	29	50	35	15
Farmers	33	67	46	54	48	52	53	47	29	51	20
Under 30	51	49	43	57	54	46	64	36	47	38	15
30–49 years	47	53	45	55	54	46	63	37	44	41	15
50 years and older	39	61	39	61	46	54	59	41	41	47	12
Protestant	37	63	37	63	38	62	55	45	35	49	16
Catholic	56	44	51	49	78	22	76	24	59	33	8
Republicans	8	92	4	96	5	95	20	80	9	86	5
Democrats	77	23	85	15	84	16	87	13	74	12	14
Independents	35	65	30	70	43	57	56	44	31	44	25
East	45	55	40	60	53	47	68	32	50	43	7
Midwest	42	58	41	59	48	52	61	39	44	47	9
South	51	49	49	51	51	49	52	48	31	36	33
West	42	58	43	57	49	51	60	40	44	49	7

* Source: *Gallup Opinion Index*, July, 1969, p. 29.

social categories and voting behavior in five presidential elections between 1952 and 1968.[27]

The most notable conclusion to be drawn from the table is that each party

[27] The behavior of Jewish voters is not shown in Table 16. In recent elections they have been among the most Democratic of all groups. A Gallup poll in 1968 reported the party identification of members of religious groups as follows: Protestant—31 percent Republican, 42 percent Democratic, 27 percent Independent; Catholic—18 percent Republican, 55 percent Democratic, 27 percent Independent; Jewish—7 percent Republican, 69 percent Democratic, 24 percent Independent. The proportion of Protestants who identify as Democrats is heavily influenced by the Democratic South; if the analysis is confined to northern states, Protestants are more likely to regard themselves as Republicans than as Democrats. *Gallup Opinion Index, Report No. 38*, 1968, p. 2.

enjoys within the electorate a set of relatively loyal followings. In election after election the Democratic party has received strong, sometimes overwhelming, support from members of the working class, Negroes, Catholics, Jews, voters with limited formal education, and younger voters. In contrast, the Republican party has ordinarily attracted a disproportionate number of voters with college educations and professional and business backgrounds. Moreover, white-collar workers, farmers, Protestants, and older voters have more often voted Republican than Democrat. On a regional basis voters in the South and the East have leaned slightly to the Democratic presidential ticket, whereas voters in the Midwest and West have been somewhat more attracted to the Republican presidential ticket.

The evidence on the voting behavior of social groups must be treated warily. The tendency of Catholics to vote Democratic, for example, is undoubtedly due more to their historical association with Democratic politics (particularly in Eastern cities) and to their socioeconomic status than it is to any factors associated with their religion. One study has shown that when the "life situation" of Catholics—for example, their socioeconomic status, education, or place of residence—is controlled, the distinctiveness of their voting behavior virtually disappears; in other words, Catholic voters are not much more likely to vote Democratic than other voters who have similar social characteristics. By contrast, union members, Negroes, and Jews vote significantly more Democratic than other individuals who occupy essentially the same life situation.[28] For individuals in these groups it is clear that membership exerts an important influence on voting behavior—in this case promoting the likelihood that they will vote Democratic.

In yet another respect the significance of group voting behavior is easy to misinterpret. The party strategist who leans too heavily on the data showing group performance may be tempted to play martial airs designed mainly to stir the followings ordinarily loyal to his party. There are, after all, a number of groups strongly identified with one or the other of the two parties. However, candidates and strategists seldom make the mistake of concentrating their appeals on narrow sectors of the electorate, no matter how attractive the possibilities may seem. The other great truth in Table 16 is that, despite the special orientations of certain groups and interests toward the parties, the parties as a whole are remarkably heterogeneous.[29] Although manual workers are dominantly Democratic, they are not exclusively Democratic. Typically, in recent presidential elections, at least one-third of the manual workers have voted Republican. A similar story can be told of those voters with professional and business backgrounds; although they are much more likely to vote Republican than Democratic, they cannot be taken for granted. In a typical

[28] Campbell *et al.*, *The American Voter*, pp. 301–306.
[29] For a study that examines the relationship between social class and party voting, see Robert R. Alford, *Party and Society* (Chicago: Rand McNally, 1963).

5

The Congressional Party and the Formation of Public Policy

The tasks that confront the American major party are formidably ambitious. From one perspective the party is a wide-ranging electoral agency organized in such a way as to make a credible bid for power. Here and there a party organization is so stunted and devitalized that it is seldom able to organize an authentic effort to win office. Elections may go by default to the dominant party as the second party struggles merely to stay in business. But throughout most of the country the parties compete on fairly even terms—if not for certain offices or in certain districts at least for some offices or in the state at large. Presidential elections, of course, are vigorously contested virtually everywhere. As electoral organizations the parties recruit candidates, organize campaigns, develop issues, and mobilize voters. The typical voter gets his best glimpse of the workings of party when he observes the "party-in-the-electorate" during political campaigns.

From another perspective, the party is a collection of officeholders who share, in some measure, common values and policy orientations. In the broadest sense its mission is to take hold of government, to identify national problems and priorities, and to work for their settlement or achievement. In a narrower sense the task of the "party-in-the-government" is to consolidate and fulfill promises made to the electorate during the campaign. How it is organized to do this and how it does it is the concern of this chapter. The focus centers on the party in Congress.

Party Representation in Congress

The critical variable in the election of members of Congress is their party affiliation. As discussed in Chapter 2, a substantial majority of House and Senate seats ordinarily are not competitive, with the result that the same party wins election after election in the district or state. It is not uncommon, in fact, for House and Senate elections to go uncontested because one party is so thoroughly dominant. Throughout much of the country, Democratic districts produce Democratic legislators and Republican districts produce Republican

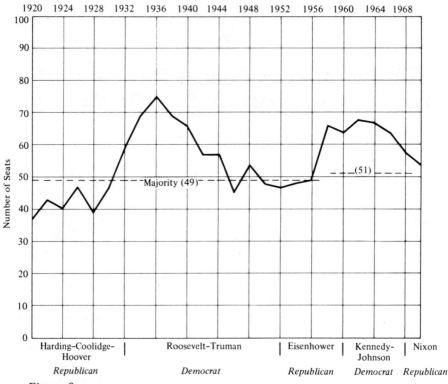

Figure 8
Democratic Strength in the U.S. Senate, 1920–1970

legislators—ordinarily without much regard for the qualifications of the candidates or without the intrusion of startling issues or events. Who wins and who loses in American elections is influenced more by the party affiliation of candidates than by any other factor.

Figures 8 and 9 depict the fortunes of the parties in congressional races over the fifty-year period from 1920 to 1970. Two central conclusions emerge. First, with few exceptions since 1932 the Democratic party has held comfortable majorities in Congress. The high point of Democratic dominance occurred in 1936 when over 75 percent of the members of both houses were Democrats. Second, the capacity of the Republican party to win presidential elections has not extended to Congress. The Republican party controlled the House by a slim margin from 1952 to 1954 and broke even in the Senate during the same period. During the remaining six years of the Eisenhower Administration both houses of Congress were held by the Democrats, at times by lopsided margins. Despite the Republican presidential victory in 1968, both houses remained safely Democratic. A massive campaign effort on behalf of many Republican candidates by President Richard Nixon and Vice-Presi-

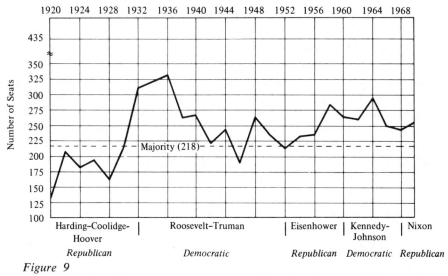

Figure 9
Democratic Strength in U.S. House of Representatives,
1920–1970

dent Spiro Agnew in the 1970 congressional election failed to improve the party's position in Congress—a gain of two seats by Republicans in the Senate was offset by a loss of nine seats in the House. Given the prevailing pattern of party allegiance in the electorate (see Chapter 4), the prospects are strong that Republican Presidents will be faced with Democratic majorities in Congress. As a result their success in getting their legislative programs adopted is likely to turn on their ability, and that of the legislative leaders of their party, to forge and maintain effective biparty coalitions.

Party membership is not only the most important variable in determining who is elected to Congress but also the most important variable in governing members' behavior once they have taken office. The fact that party lines collapse on certain kinds of issues that come before Congress does not alter the general proposition that party affiliation is the principal determinant of legislative voting. This matter will be considered following an analysis of the character and quality of party organization in Congress.

Party Organization in Congress

Party Conferences In the broadest sense the governing agency of each party in each house is the conference or caucus. Each member elected to Congress automatically becomes a member of his party's caucus. Although this agency theoretically dominates party affairs, in fact its functions are sharply constricted, confined mainly to the selection of such party leaders as the Speaker of the House, the floor leaders and whips, and the chairmen of the policy committees. For a short period during the early twentieth century—notably during the Wilson Administration—the majority party caucus was extraordinarily powerful. Members were expected to be loyal to their party, and caucus decisions to bind the members occurred frequently on major legislation. After World War I disillusionment with the caucus became manifest as members increasingly questioned the right of the caucus to bind them to a course of action. Today the caucuses meet infrequently, and more important, their impact on party policy and members' voting behavior has become negligible. The weakness of the caucus is not hard to explain: each party is a mass of oppositions, tensions, and contradictions. No single voice can speak for the party, and no central agency can dominate it.

The Speaker of the House   The most powerful party leader in Congress is the Speaker of the House. In the early twentieth century the Speaker's powers were virtually beyond limit, the House virtually his private domain. It is scarcely an exaggeration to say that legislation the Speaker favored was adopted and that legislation he opposed was lost. The despotic rule of Speaker "Uncle Joe" Cannon eventually proved his undoing. A coalition of Democrats and rebellious Republicans was formed in 1910 to challenge the leadership of Cannon. After a struggle of many months they succeeded in instituting a number of rules changes to curb the Speaker's powers. He was removed from membership on the Rules Committee (of which he had been chairman), his power to appoint and remove members and chairmen of the standing committees was eliminated, and his power to recognize (or not to recognize) members was limited. Although the "revolution of 1910–1911" fundamentally altered the formal powers of the Speaker, it did not render the office impotent. Since then, a succession of Speakers—men disposed to negotiate rather than to command—has helped to rebuild the powers of the office. What a Speaker like Joseph G. Cannon (1903–1911) secured through autocratic rule, today's Speakers secure through persuasion and the astute exploitation of the bargaining advantages that are inherent in their positions.

The Speaker's formal powers are wide-ranging though not especially significant in themselves. He is, of course, the presiding officer of the House; in this capacity he announces the order of business, puts questions to a vote, refers bills to committees, rules on points of order, interprets the rules, recognizes members who desire the floor, and appoints members to select and conference committees. In addition, he has the right to vote and enter floor debate; ordinarily he exercises these opportunities only in the case of major, closely contested issues.[1]

[1] The Speaker's formal counterpart in the Senate is the Vice-President. His role is simply that of presiding officer, since he is not a member of the body, cannot enter debate, and is permitted to vote only in the case of a tie. His influence on the legislative process is ordinarily insignificant.

Although difficult to delineate with precision, the informal powers of the Speaker are far more impressive. As the foremost leader of his party in Congress he is at the center of critical information and policy-making systems. No one is in a better position than the Speaker to obtain and disseminate information, to shape strategies, or to advance or frustrate the careers of members. Perhaps the principal "tangible preferment" the Speaker has at his disposal is the influence he can exert to secure favorable committee assignments for members of the majority party. Having the good will of the Speaker is important to members of his party anxious to move ahead in the House. The following analysis by Randall Ripley describes the structure of the Speaker's influence:

> His personal traits influence his ability to deal with members of his party. The one constant element is the importance of his showing trust in and respect for individual members of his party. A smile or nod of the head from the Speaker can bolster a member's ego and lead him to seek further evidences of favor. Being out of favor hurts the individual's pride, and may be noticed by his colleagues. Most Speakers have had an instinct for knowing their loyal followers on legislative matters. Others have either kept records themselves or made frequent use of whip polls and official records to inform themselves about the relative loyalty of their members. Speakers have been able to convey critical information to members on a person-to-person basis, often with the help of the Parliamentarian. They have also encouraged their floor leaders and whip organizations to become collectors and purveyors of information on a larger scale. Particularly useful to a number of Speakers has been an informal gathering of intimates and friends of both parties to discuss the course of business in the House. Through such discussions, Speakers have been able to keep themselves informed of developments in the House and, at the same time, convey their desires to other members invited to attend.[2]

The Floor Leaders   In addition to the Speaker of the House, the key figures in the congressional party organizations are the House and Senate floor leaders, who are chosen by party caucuses in their respective chambers. The floor leaders serve as the principal spokesmen for party positions and interests and as mediaries in both intraparty and interparty negotiations. The floor leaders of the party that controls the presidency also serve as links between the President and his congressional party. Because floor leaders are obliged to play several roles at the same time—for example, as representatives of both the congressional party and the President—it is not surprising that role conflicts develop. Serving the interests of his congressional party colleagues or perhaps those of his constituents is anything but a guarantee that he will be serving presidential interests.

[2] Randall B. Ripley, *Party Leaders in the House of Representatives* (Washington, D.C.: The Brookings Institution, 1967), pp. 23–24.

The floor leader has a potpourri of informal, middling powers. Their availability does not insure that he can, in fact, lead his colleagues or strongly shape the legislative program. By and large, his influence is based upon his willingness and talent to exploit these powers steadily and imaginatively in his relations with other members. He can, if he chooses, influence the allocation of committee assignments (not only rewarding individual members but also shaping the ideological makeup of the committees), help members to advance legislation of particular interest to them, assist members in securing larger appropriations for their committees or subcommittees, play a major role in debate, intercede with the President or executive agencies on behalf of members (perhaps to assist their efforts to secure a federal project in their state or district), make important information available to members, help members to secure campaign money from a congressional campaign committee, campaign on behalf of individual members, and focus the attention of the communications media on the contributions of members. Much of the influence of the floor leader, like that of the Speaker, is derived from informal powers, in particular from opportunities afforded him to advance or protect the careers of party colleagues. In solving problems for them and in making their positions more secure, he increases the prospects of gaining their support on critical questions. By the same token, the floor leader can in some measure hamper the careers of those members who continually refuse to go along with him. At the center of the active floor leader's powers is the capacity to manipulate rewards and punishments.

An important function and a major source of power for the majority floor leader, particularly in the Senate, is that of controlling the scheduling of bill consideration on the floor. In the House the Rules Committee dominates the process of controlling the agenda. However pedestrian the scheduling function may sound, it is a surprisingly important source of power. The majority leader who fails to keep his lines of communication clear, who misjudges the sentiments of members, who neglects to consolidate his majority by winning over undecided members or by propping up wavering members, or who picks the wrong time to call up a bill, can easily go down to defeat. Prospective majorities are much more tenuous and much more easily upset than might be supposed. Support can be rapidly lost as a result of poor communications, missed opportunities for negotiation and compromise, and bad timing. The effective leader builds his power base by tending to the shop, by ordering priorities, by having a sense of detail that overlooks nothing, by taking account of the demands placed upon members, by sensing the mood of congressional opinion (especially that of key members), and by exhibiting skill in splicing together the legislative elements necessary to fashion a majority.

The principal power of the floor leader is the power of persuasion. As a former Democratic leader of the Senate, Lyndon Johnson, has observed, ". . . the only real power available to the leader is the power of persuasion.

There is no patronage; no power to discipline; no authority to fire Senators like a President can fire his members of Cabinet."[3] To be effective in persuasion, a leader must know the members well, know what they want and what they will settle for and what concessions they can make and what concessions they cannot make, given their constituencies. The critical importance of such information requires the leader to develop a reliable communications network within his party. But more than that, he requires good lines of communication into the other party in order to pick up support here and there when elements of his own party appear likely to wander off the reservation. Other things being equal, members prefer to support their leader and the party position rather than the opposing forces. The task of the leader is to find reasons for them to do so and conditions under which they can.

The development of a legislative program requires the majority leader to work closely with the key leaders in his party, particularly the chairmen of the major committees. As Lyndon Johnson observed during his tenure as Senate majority leader, "You must understand why the committee took certain actions and why certain judgments were formed."[4] His successor, Mike Mansfield, has said: "I'm not the leader, really. They don't do what I tell them. I do what they tell me. . . . The brains are in the committees."[5] The effective leader works with the resources available—in essence, the power of persuasion. Relations between the leader and the committee chairmen are never characterized by a one-way flow of mandates. On the contrary, the leader must be acutely sensitive to the interests of the chairmen, adept at recognizing their political problems, and flexible in his negotiations with them. Bargaining is the key characteristic of the relationships between the majority leader and the committee chairmen.

It is one thing to say that floor leaders must negotiate with committee chairmen and quite another to suggest that committee chairmen dominate the bargaining process. Research on the 81st Congress by David Truman calls into question the proposition that the seniority leaders—the committee chairmen and the ranking minority members—are the principal custodians of congressional power. His test of their relative influence is based on an analysis of roll call votes on the floor. There are many votes on which the floor leaders and the seniority leaders take opposite sides. Truman's study indicates that when such divisions occur, the floor leader is usually found on the winning side of the vote. An even better test of the floor leader's influence is that when these voting splits develop, the members of the chairman's own committee are

[3] "Leadership: An Interview with Senate Leader Lyndon Johnson," *U.S. News & World Report*, June 27, 1960, p. 88. Reprinted from *U.S. News & World Report*, Copyright 1960 by U.S. News & World Report. See also Ralph K. Huitt, "Democratic Party Leadership in the Senate," *American Political Science Review*, LV (June 1961), pp. 333–344.

[4] "Leadership: An Interview with Senate Leader Lyndon Johnson," p. 90.

[5] *The New York Times*, July 17, 1961, p. 11.

more likely to take their voting cues from the leader than from their chairman. The data suggest, writes Truman, that the floor leaders ". . ..were not at the mercy of the seniority leaders and they did, with varying degrees of effectiveness, act as if they were the trustees of the party's record."[6] This study makes a good case for the argument that the "formal" and the "real" leadership of the congressional party is ordinarily lodged in the office of the floor leader, especially on the majority side.

What has been said thus far suggests that there are several important constraints that shape the position of the floor leader. The leader is not free to fashion his role as he might like to see it. The limited range of powers available to him, his personality, his relationship to the President, and his skills in bargaining all affect in some measure the definition of his role. Moreover, no two leaders are likely to perceive the leader role in exactly the same light. In addition, the nature of the leader's position is strongly influenced by the nature of the legislative parties. The evidence is that the persistent cleavages present within both parties make it necessary for the leaders to occupy the role of middleman. The leader is a middleman in the sense that he is more or less steadily involved in negotiations with all major elements within the party and also a middleman in terms of his voting record.[7] In the passage of much legislation the test is not so much the wisdom of the decision but its political feasibility. A leader identified with an extreme group within his party would find it difficult to work out the kinds of compromises necessary to put together a majority. The leader is first and foremost a broker. Candidates for leadership positions whose voting records place them on the ideological edges of their party are less likely to be elected than those whose voting records fall within the central range of party opinion.

The Whips   Another unit in the party structure of Congress is the whip organization. Party whips are selected in each house by the floor leaders or by other party agencies. A number of assistant whips are required in the House of Representatives because of the large size of the body. Working to enhance the efforts of the leadership, the whips carry on a number of important functions. They attempt to learn how members intend to vote on legislation, relay information from party leaders to individual members, work to insure that a large number of "friendly" members will be present at the time of voting, and attempt to win the support of those party members who are in opposition, or likely to be in opposition, to the leadership. The whips are also charged with discovering why members are opposed to certain legislation and how it could be changed to gain their support. The central importance of the whip organization is that it forms a communications link between the

[6] David B. Truman, *The Congressional Party* (New York: Wiley, 1959), p. 246.
[7] See Truman, *The Congressional Party*, especially pp. 106–116 and 205–208.

party leadership and its rank-and-file members. The intelligence and leverage the whips supply is sometimes the difference between victory and defeat on a major issue. The relatively decentralized character of congressional party organization has made the whip function indispensable to all efforts to achieve party unity.[8] On some issues, of course, no amount of activity on the part of the leadership can bring recalcitrant members into the fold.

The Policy Committees   There have been few proposals for congressional reform that have received as much attention as those designed to strengthen the role of political parties in the legislative process. The Joint Committee on the Organization of Congress recommended in its 1946 report that policy committees be created for the purpose of formulating the basic policies of the two parties. Although this provision was later stricken from the reorganization bill, the Senate independently created such committees in 1947. The House Republicans established a policy committee in 1949, though it did not become fully active for another decade.[9] On the other hand, for one reason or another the House Democrats have never found it appropriate to create such a committee.

The high promise of the policy committees as agencies for enhancing party responsibility for legislative programs has never been realized. Neither party leaders nor rank-and-file members have been agreed on the functions of the policy committees. There is not much exaggeration in the observation that the policy committees are "policy" committees in name only. The policy committees in the Senate ". . . have never been 'policy' bodies, in the sense of considering and investigating alternatives of public policy, and they have never put forth an over-all congressional party program. The committees do not assume leadership in drawing up a general legislative program . . . and only rarely have the committees labeled their decisions as 'party policies.' "[10]

It is not surprising that the policy committees have been unable to function effectively as agencies for the development of overall party programs. An authoritative policy committee would constitute a major threat to the scattered and relatively independent centers of power within Congress. The seniority leaders who preside over the committee system would undoubtedly find their influence over legislation diminished if the policy committees were to assume a central role in defining party positions. Not only would the independence of

[8] See a study by Randall B. Ripley, "The Party Whip Organizations in the United States House of Representatives," *American Political Science Review*, LVIII (September 1964), pp. 561–576.

[9] For a detailed study of this committee, see Charles O. Jones, *Party and Policy-Making: The House Republican Policy Committee* (New Brunswick, N.J.: Rutgers University Press, 1964).

[10] Hugh A. Bone, "An Introduction to the Senate Policy Committees," *American Political Science Review*, L (June 1956), p. 352.

the committee system be affected adversely, but many individual members would suffer an erosion of power. Had the policy committees functioned as planned, a major reshuffling of power in Congress would have resulted. To the men who hold the keys to congressional power, this is scarcely an appealing idea. However attractive the proposal for centralized committees empowered to speak for the parties in Congress, they are altogether unlikely to emerge so long as the parties themselves are decentralized and fragmented, composed of members who represent a wide variety of constituencies and ideological positions.

Although the lack of internal party agreement prevents the policy committees from functioning in a policy-shaping capacity, it does not render them useless. Both parties require forums for the discussion of issues and for the negotiation of compromises, and for these activities the policy committees are well designed. Moreover, the staffs of the committees have proved helpful for individual members seeking research assistance. Most important, the policy committees have served as a communications channel between the party leaders and their memberships. The policy committees are an ambitious attempt to come to terms with the nagging problem of party disunity. If generally they have failed in this respect, they have nonetheless succeeded in other respects. As clearinghouses for the exchange of party information and as agencies for the reconciliation of at least some intraparty differences, they have made useful contributions.

Informal Party Groups   In addition to the formal party units in Congress, there are several informal party organizations that meet more or less regularly to discuss legislation, strategy, and other questions of common interest. Among these organizations are the Democratic Study Group, the Chowder and Marching Club (Republican), the Acorns (Republican), the S.O.S. (Republican), and the Wednesday Club (Republican)—all House groups. The best-known, largest, and most effective of these organizations is the Democratic Study Group. Formed in 1959 by liberal Democrats as a counterbloc to the southern wing of the party, the DSG has grown steadily in numbers and in influence. In recent Congresses the DSG has had a membership of 125 to 150 members, elected leaders, a whip system, a full-time staff, and a campaign unit to assist in fund-raising and campaign development. The distinguishing features of the DSG are its preoccupation with issues and its liberal bias.[11]

---

[11] For analysis of the role and functions of informal party groups in Congress, see Kenneth Kofmehl, "The Institutionalization of a Voting Bloc," *Western Political Quarterly*, XVII (June 1964), pp. 256–272, and Sven Groennings, "The Wednesday Group in the House of Representatives: A Structural-Functional Analysis," a paper delivered at the annual meeting of the Midwest Political Science Association, Chicago, 1970.

Factors Influencing the Success of Party Leaders The cohesiveness of the parties in Congress can never be taken for granted. The independence of the committees and their chairmen, the rudimentary powers of elected leaders, the importance of constituency pressures, the influence of political interest groups, and the disposition of members to respond to parochial impulses—all, at one time or another, contribute to the fragmentation of power in Congress and to the erosion of party unity. The member who ignores leadership cues and requests or is oblivious to them, or who in fact builds a career as a party maverick, is far more common than might be supposed. There are few weapons in the leadership arsenal that can be used to bring refractory members into line.

Recent research on the Democratic party in the House of Representatives by Lewis Froman and Randall Ripley identifies a number of conditions under which leadership influence on legislative decisions will either be promoted or inhibited.[12] In the first place, leadership success is likely to be contingent upon a high degree of agreement among the leaders themselves. Ordinarily the Speaker, majority leader, and whip will be firm supporters of their President's legislative program; frequently, however, other key leaders, such as committee chairmen, will be allied with opponents. When unity among the leaders breaks down, prospects for success fall sharply. Second, leadership success in gathering the party together tends to be affected by the nature of the issue under consideration—specifically, whether it is procedural or substantive. On procedural issues (for example, election of the Speaker, adoption of rules, motions to adjourn), party cohesion is ordinarily much higher than on issues that involve substantive policy. Third, the efforts of party leaders are most likely to be successful on issues that do not have high visibility to the general public. In the usual pattern, conflicting pressures emerge when issues gain visibility, and the leaders must commit greater resources to keep their ranks intact.

In the fourth place, the visibility of the action to be taken will have bearing on the inclination of members to follow the leadership. Not all forms of voting, for example, are equally visible. Roll call votes on final passage of measures are highly visible—the member's "record" on a public question is firmly established at this point. Voting with the leadership at this stage may seem to the member to pose too great a risk. On the other hand, supporting the leadership in committee or on a key amendment is less risky because the actions are not as easily brought into public focus. Fifth, and perhaps most important, members are most likely to vote with their party when the issue at stake does not stir up opposition in their constituencies. Party leaders know full well that they cannot count on the support of members who feel that they are

---

[12] See Lewis Froman and Randall Ripley, "Conditions for Party Leadership: The Case of the House Democrats," *American Political Science Review*, LIX (March 1965), pp. 52–63.

under the thumb of constituents on a particular issue—for example, southern members on certain questions relating to civil rights. Finally, support for the leadership is likely to be dependent upon the activity of the state delegations. Leadership victories are more likely to result when individual state delegations are not involved in bargaining with leaders over specific demands.

These conditions, then, comprise the background against which leadership efforts to mold their party as a unit take place. Party loyalty, it should be emphasized, is more than a veneer. By and large, members prefer to stay "regular," to go along with their party colleagues. But they will not queue up in support of their leaders if the conditions appear "wrong," if apparently there is more to be lost than gained by following the leadership. Members guard their careers by taking frequent soundings within their constituencies and among their colleagues and by making careful calculations as to the consequences that are likely to flow from their decisions.

National Party Agencies and the Congressional Parties

In theory, the supreme governing body of the party between one national convention and the next is the national committee, which is composed of representatives from each of the states. In the best of all worlds, from the perspective of those who believe in party unity and responsibility, there would be close and continuing relationships between the national committee of each party and fellow party members in Congress. Out of such associations, presumably, would come coherent party policies and a heightened sense of responsibility among congressmen for developing a legislative program consistent with the promises of the party platform. In point of fact, however, the tone and mood that dominate relations between the national committees and the congressional parties are as likely to be characterized by suspicion as by cooperation. Congressional leaders in particular are little disposed to follow the cues that emanate from the national committees or, for that matter, from any other national party agency. When, for example, the Democratic Advisory Council was created in 1956 as an agency to focus attention on the party's program (as an alternative to that of the Eisenhower Administration), many Democrats in Congress, including the leadership, refused to join. They recognized that DAC membership might inhibit their freedom of action in Congress, in some measure committing them to legislative programs deemed unacceptable.[13]

[13] In 1969 the Democratic party formed a group similar to the DAC, calling it the Democratic Policy Council. At the time of its formation the Democratic National Chairman made it clear that the Council would not intrude on congressional prerogatives; short-term issues were to be left to the party in Congress. Only five Democratic members of Congress, and none of the leaders, were selected for membership on the Council's twenty-member executive committee. The Council was created to generate ideas on policy questions and to plan for future elections.

Not only do national party leaders have a minimal impact on congressional decision-making but they are also largely excluded from the nominating process for congressional candidates. They seldom engage in negotiations with state and local party leaders on matters relating to congressional nominations. The reason for this is simply that state and local leaders, with considerable power in their own right, resent national interference in what is regarded as a state or local party function. Occasionally an intrepid President has sought to influence congressional nominations, as Franklin D. Roosevelt did in 1938. Disturbed by mounting opposition to his program in Congress, Roosevelt publicly endorsed the primary opponents of certain prominent anti-New Deal incumbent Democrats. As it turned out, nearly all of the lawmakers marked for defeat won easily, much to the chagrin of the President. Twelve years later President Harry S. Truman met the same fate when he endorsed a candidate in the Democratic senatorial primary in Missouri; the state party organization rallied to the other side, and the President lost. Although a few presidential "purges" have succeeded, most attempts have failed. The lesson seems evident: congressional nominations are regarded as "local" matters, and the President who attempts to influence these nominations runs a good risk of suffering both public embarrassment and sharp congressional criticism.

The national party is concerned with the election of congressmen who are broadly sympathetic to its traditional policy orientations and its party platform. In counterpoise, local party organizations aim to guarantee their own survival as independent units. Occasional conflict between the two is predictable. The principal consequence of local control over congressional nominations is that all manner of men and women get elected to Congress, those who find it easy to accept national party goals and those who are almost wholly out of step with the national party. The failure of party unity in Congress is due as much as anything to the folkway that congressional nominations are local questions to be settled by local politicians and voters according to preferences they alone establish.

Do the Parties Differ on Public Policies?

Party affiliation is the cutting edge of congressional elections. Ordinarily there are few surprises on election day: Democratic candidates win where they are expected to win, and Republican candidates win where they are expected to win. The public at large may continue to believe that each election poses an opportunity for the "outs" to replace the "ins," but in fact this happens infrequently. The chief threat to an incumbent legislator is a landslide presidential vote for the other party, one so great that congressional candidates on the winning presidential ticket are lifted into office on the strength of the presidential candidate's coattails. Even landslide votes, however, do not disturb the great majority of congressional races.

If party affiliation largely determines which men and women go to Congress, does it also significantly influence their behavior once in office? The answer for most legislators—for majorities within each party—is yes. Party affiliation, we noted earlier, is the most important single variable in predicting how members will respond to questions that come before them. Indeed, the key fact to be known about any member is the party to which he belongs —it influences his choice of friends, his membership in groups, his relations with lobbies, his relations with other members and the leadership, and most important, his policy orientations. Party loyalty does not govern the behavior of members, but neither is it a factor taken lightly.

The proportion of roll call votes in Congress in which the parties are firmly opposed to each other is not particularly large. A study of selected congressional sessions between 1921 and 1967 shows that the number of "party votes" that occur in the House of Representatives has declined markedly over the years. Between 1921 and 1948, about 17 percent of the House roll call votes were "party votes"—votes in which 90 percent of the voting membership of one party opposed 90 percent of the voting membership of the other party. In the usual House sessions since 1950, party votes have numbered about 6 or 7 percent of the total. The "90 percent vs. 90 percent" standard is, of course, an exceedingly rigorous test of party voting. If the standard is relaxed to "50 percent vs. 50 percent" the proportion of party votes rises sharply. Typically, during the 1950s and 1960s, about one-half of the session roll call votes found party majorities arrayed against each other. Although party voting is less common today than in earlier periods, important issues are often at stake when party lines form. In general, Democrats have been much more likely than Republicans to support a low tariff, federal programs to assist agriculture, expanded health and welfare programs, legislation advantageous to labor and low-income groups, government regulation of business, and a larger role for the federal government.[14]

[14] See Edward V. Schneier's revised version of a classic study by Julius Turner, *Party and Constituency: Pressures on Congress* (Baltimore: Johns Hopkins Press, 1970), especially Chapters 2 and 3, from which the data of this paragraph were drawn. For another study of the differences between Democrats and Republicans in the period from 1947 to 1962, see David R. Mayhew, *Party Loyalty Among Congressmen* (Cambridge, Mass.: Harvard University Press, 1966). His analysis of the parties' performances during this period is instructive: "It can be said that the Democratic party in these years was transcendently a party of 'inclusive' compromise. . . . Some congressmen wanted dams, others wanted mineral subsidies, others wanted area redevelopment funds, others wanted housing projects, still others wanted farm subsidies. As a result, the House Democratic leadership could serve as an instrument for mobilizing support among all Democrats for the programs of Democrats with particular interests. 'Indifferent' Democratic congressmen frequently backed such programs 'even against the debatable best interests of the people of their own communities.' Republicans who characterized the Democratic party as a 'gravy train' were quite right. . . . The essential point is that the program of the Democratic party in the House—of party leaders and of party majorities—was arrived at by adding together the programs of different elements of the

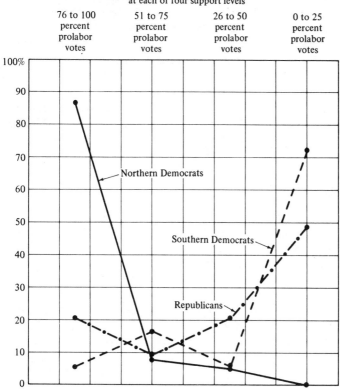

Percentage of each party group voting prolabor positions
at each of four support levels

| 76 to 100 percent prolabor votes | 51 to 75 percent prolabor votes | 26 to 50 percent prolabor votes | 0 to 25 percent prolabor votes |

Figure 10
Support for Labor Legislation by Party and Section,
U.S. Senate, 91st Congress, 1st Session

Source of data: *Congressional Quarterly Weekly Report*, XXVIII (February 20, 1970), p. 569. Each member of the Senate is ranked in terms of the percentage of votes which he cast in accord with the position of the AFL-CIO Committee on Political Education.

The Parties and Liberal-Labor Legislation   The policy orientations of the parties in Congress today are not markedly different from those they held

---

party. . . . *Whenever possible*, most Republican congressmen opposed federal spending programs and championed policies favored by business. Thus, whereas 'interested' minorities in the Democratic party typically supported each other's programs, each 'interested' minority in the Republican party stood alone. The Republican leadership responded to the legislative demands of each minority by mobilizing the rest of the party to oppose them. City Republicans joined colleagues from the traditional 'heartland' in voting against farm bills; Farm Belt members joined members from the 'heartland' in opposing housing bills; almost everyone answered the party call in voting on labor or public power questions." Reprinted by permission of the publishers from David R. Mayhew's *Party Loyalty Among Congressmen*, Cambridge, Mass.: Harvard University Press, 1966, pp. 150–153.

during the New Deal-Fair Deal eras. Figures 10 and 11 depict the positions of the parties (and the wings within them) on proposals of interest to the AFL-CIO in the first session of the 91st Congress. A member voting in accordance with AFL-CIO positions would have supported bills to provide for an expansion of the food stamp program for poverty-level families, an increase in funds for urban renewal, tax reform providing for an increase in personal exemptions, an increase in appropriations for the Office of Economic Opportunity, a limitation on farm subsidy payments to $20,000 annually for any one recipient, and an increase in appropriations for programs of the Office of Education. Similarly, he would have opposed bills to deny tax exemptions

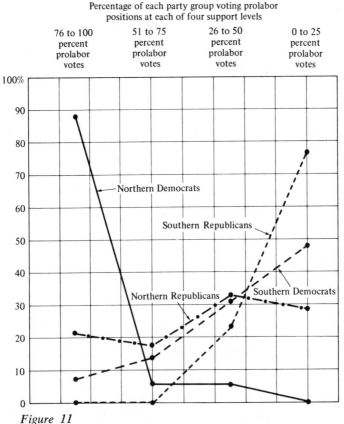

Figure 11
Support for Labor Legislation by Party and Section,
U.S. House of Representatives, 91st Congress,
1st Session

Source of data: *Congressional Quarterly Weekly Report*, XXVIII (February 20, 1970), pp. 570–571. Each member of the House is ranked in terms of the percentage of votes which he cast in accord with the position of the AFL-CIO Committee on Political Education.

for tax-exempt organizations that support political activities such as voter registration drives, to limit extension of the Elementary and Secondary Education Act, to curtail the Peace Corps Act, to change the Electoral College by providing for the election of electors from congressional districts, and to make the antipoverty program a state program.[15]

A glance at Figures 10 and 11 will reveal two broad characteristics of congressional voting on legislation of central interest to organized labor. First, it is plain that the parties are not cohesive units in voting on liberal-labor legislation. Second, notwithstanding intraparty splits, there are substantial differences between the parties. The two largest groups in each house —northern Democrats and northern Republicans—view liberal-labor legislation from vastly different perspectives. Nearly 90 percent of the northern Democrats in each house are found at the highest support level—voting in agreement with AFL-CIO positions between 76 and 100 percent of the time —whereas only about 20 percent of the northern Republicans are at this level. Moreover, only a handful of northern Democrats are out of step with labor objectives, voting less than half the time with the AFL-CIO.[16]

The principal opponents of liberal-labor legislation in Congress are southern Democrats and southern Republicans, particularly the latter. In the House nearly 80 percent of the southern Republicans are grouped in the lowest support level (0 to 25 percent). In the Senate the legislators most likely to take a dim view of legislation endorsed by organized labor are southern Democrats. Over 70 percent of this group are lodged in the 0-25 support level.

Figure 12 offers another way of looking at the policy orientations of the congressional parties. This figure shows the range of opinion in the Senate in the 91st Congress (1st session) on issues deemed important by the liberal-oriented Americans for Democratic Action and the conservative-oriented Americans for Constitutional Action.[17] Each senator is located on the dia-

---

[15] *Congressional Quarterly Weekly Report*, XXVIII (February 20, 1970), pp. 572–576.

[16] The totals for each party group in this analysis of the House are 166 northern Democrats, 79 southern Democrats (the states of the Confederacy), 161 northern Republicans, and 26 southern Republicans. (The Speaker's seat plus two vacancies bring the total to 435.) For the Senate, the figures are 39 northern Democrats, 18 southern Democrats, and 43 Republicans.

[17] The key issues for the ADA and ACA in this Congress differ in some respects from those of the AFL-CIO. A senator voting a pro-ADA position in this session would have supported, among other things, efforts to liberalize the cloture rule (to make it easier to terminate debate), to restrict funds for the Safeguard ABM system to research and development, to provide for regular reports by the Defense Department on major contracts and for a GAO audit and reports on such contracts, to reduce funds for a new Air Force bomber, to reduce the oil and gas depletion allowance, to reject President Nixon's nomination of Clement Haynsworth as an Associate Justice of the Supreme Court, to increase Social Security payments, and to provide supplemental appropriations for programs of the U.S. Commissioner of Education and the Department of Health,

gram according to the percentage of votes that he cast that were in agreement with the positions of each political interest group. Senator Gaylord Nelson (D., Wis.), for example, scored 100 percent on the ADA scale and 0 percent on the ACA scale. At the other pole, Senator Edward Gurney (R., Fla.) and Senator Strom Thurmond (R., S.C.) had a 93 percent support score on ACA positions and 0 percent on ADA positions.

Figure 12 reinforces our earlier conclusions. Despite the party-in-disarray quality that emerges in the Senate scattergram, it is nevertheless clear that significant differences separate the majorities of the two parties. A majority of the Republican senators are found on the right-hand side of the diagram, indicating their agreement with the ACA, while a majority of Democratic senators are lodged on the left-hand side, indicating their agreement with the ADA. The "deviant" behavior of party members is largely confined to certain "wings" in each party. A strong majority of southern Democrats are clustered well over on the "conservative" side of the diagram; similarly, a number of Republicans from populous eastern states—for example, Clifford Case (N.J.), Jacob Javits (N.Y.), Edward Brooke (Mass.), Charles Mathias (Md.), and Richard Schweiker (Pa.)—are shown to be more supportive of ADA than ACA positions. Only three northern Democrats—two from Nevada and one from West Virginia—have higher ACA than ADA support scores. Finally, viewed from an overall perspective, the Senate emerges as an institution more likely to support liberal public policies than conservative ones.

Biparty Coalitions   Of all the problems that confront the legislative party, none is more persistent or difficult than that of maintaining party unity. There are members who assiduously ignore the requests and entreaties of leaders,

Figure 12
Support of Positions Held by Americans for
Democratic Action and by Americans for Constitutional
Action by Each Senator, in Percentages, 91st Congress,
1st Session. Data are Derived from the *Congressional
Quarterly Weekly Report,* XXVIII, February 20,
1970, p. 569

Education and Welfare. On the other hand, a senator voting in accordance with ACA positions would have opposed bills on resolutions to increase the permanent debt ceiling, to authorize certain funds for the International Development Association, to eliminate the $20,000 ceiling on yearly subsidy payments to individual farmers, to prevent funds from being used on the Safeguard ABM system, to expand the food stamp program, to increase appropriations for urban renewal, and to increase appropriations for OEO, among other things. For a complete listing of the ADA and ACA positions, see the *Congressional Quarterly Weekly Report,* XXVIII (February 20, 1970), pp. 572–574.

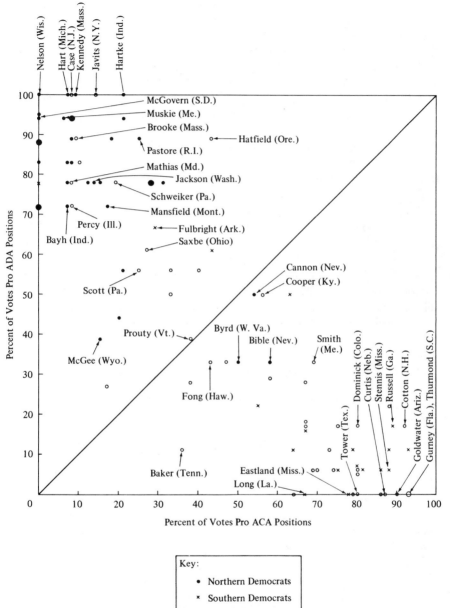

Key:

- • Northern Democrats
- × Southern Democrats
- ○ Republicans

others who cling tenaciously to constituency lines without pausing to consider the requirements of party, and still others who seek to tailor party measures to the specifications of those parochial interests to which they respond. The party is a repository for divergent claims and preferences. Getting it to act as a collectivity is no mean feat.

The disruption of party lines leads to the formation of biparty coalitions. The most durable biparty coalition in the history of Congress has been the so-called conservative coalition—an informal league of southern Democrats and northern Republicans. Table 17 provides a statistical picture of the power held by the coalition in ten congressional sessions since 1961. In recent years the coalition has come to life on about one-fourth of the roll-call votes held during a session. More important, the coalition's successes often have been spectacular. In only two sessions over this period (1965 and 1966, the first two years of Lyndon Johnson's "Great Society") did the coalition win less than 50 percent of the roll calls on which it appeared. In five of the ten sessions the "batting average" of the coalition exceeded 60 percent.

The conservative coalition is a potent force in Congress. A wide range of issues occupy its attention. In general, it can be counted on to resist new federal spending on education and welfare or to attempt to cut the level of this spending, to support proposals to transfer federal programs to the states (for example, the effort in the 91st Congress to make the antipoverty program

Table 17
The Conservative Coalition in Congress, Appearances
and Victories, 1961–1970*

| YEAR | PERCENTAGE OF ROLL CALLS ON WHICH THE COALITION APPEARED—BOTH HOUSES** | PERCENTAGE OF COALITION VICTORIES | | |
		Both Houses	*House*	*Senate*
1961	28%	55%	74%	48%
1962	14	62	44	71
1963	17	50	67	44
1964	15	51	67	47
1965	24	33	25	39
1966	25	45	32	51
1967	20	63	73	54
1968	24	73	63	80
1969	27	68	71	67
1970	22	66	70	64

* *Congressional Quarterly Weekly Report*, January 29, 1971, p. 243.
** A "coalition roll call" is defined as any roll call on which the majority of voting southern Democrats and the majority of voting Republicans are opposed to the majority of voting northern Democrats. The Congressional Quarterly includes these states in the southern wing of the Democratic party: Ala., Ark., Fla., Ga., Ky., La., Miss., N.C., Okla., S.C., Tenn., Tex., and Va. The other thirty-seven states are classified as "northern" in this analysis.

a state program), to support the military and the Department of Defense (for example, deployment of the Safeguard antiballistic missile or construction of aircraft carriers or manned bombers), to support major business sections (for example, oil and gas tax depletion allowances), to favor military rather than economic aid to foreign countries, and to oppose certain kinds of civil rights legislation (for example, strict federal controls over voting).

The President and the Congressional Party

Presidential power appears more awesome at a distance than it does at close range. Although the Constitution awards the President a number of formal powers—for example, the power to initiate treaties, to make certain appointments, and to veto legislation—his principal day-in, day-out power is simply the power to persuade. The President who opts for an active role in the legislative process, who attempts to persuade members of Congress to accept his leadership and his program, runs up against certain obstacles in the structure of American government. Foremost among these is the separation of powers. This arrangement of "separated institutions sharing powers"[18] not only divides the formal structure of government, creating independent centers of legislative and executive authority, but it also contributes to the fragmentation of the national parties. The perspectives of those elements of the party for whom the President speaks are not necessarily the same as those for whom members of his congressional party speak. Policy that may suit one constituency may not suit another. Indeed, the chances are high that the presidential constituency and the constituencies of individual members of his party in Congress will differ in many important respects, making a certain amount of conflict between the branches inevitable.

The separation of powers is not the only constraint that faces the activist President who hopes to move Congress to adopt his program. The lack of centralized party leadership in Congress, the independent position of committees, the power of committee chairmen, the paucity of sanctions to apply to wayward legislators, and the parochial cast in congressional perceptions of policy problems all converge to limit presidential influence. Moreover, electoral arrangements and electoral behavior may make executive leadership difficult. Off-year elections are nearly always more damaging to the President's party than they are to the out-party. In off-year elections from 1926 to 1970, for example, the President's party gained seats in only one House election (1934) and in only three Senate elections (1934, 1962, and 1970).

---

[18] Richard E. Neustadt, *Presidential Power: The Politics of Leadership* (New York: Wiley, 1960), p. 33.

Losses are often severe; the Democratic party emerged from the 1966 election with forty-seven fewer seats in the House, and the Republican party lost forty-seven House seats in the 1958 election.

Finally, the root of the President's legislative difficulties may lie with the voters themselves. The election that produces a President of one party may yield a Congress dominated by the other party (for example, the election of 1968) or one influenced by a different ideological coloration. James Sundquist's analysis of John F. Kennedy's congressional miseries is instructive:

> [It] is neither fair nor accurate to blame the failure of the Kennedy domestic program in the Eighty-seventh Congress primarily upon congressional organization or procedure—the power of the reformed House Rules Committee, the seniority system, or any other of Congress' internal processes. The failure of Congress to enact the Kennedy program is chargeable, rather, to the simple fact that the voters who elected Kennedy did not send to Congress enough supporters of his program. His razor-thin popular majority was reflected in a Congress formally Democratic but actually narrowly balanced between activists and conservatives. If the machinery of both houses had been entirely controlled by supporters of the Kennedy program, that in itself would not have changed the convictions of the members so as to produce a dependable administration majority. The machinery might have been used more effectively to coerce Democratic congressmen into voting in opposition to their convictions— but that is another matter.[19]

So many words have been written about the role of the President as "chief legislator" that it is easy to lose sight of the fact that members of Congress have power in their own right. Although it is clear that in recent decades the initiative in the generation of legislation has shifted to the President, it is also true that Congress remains one of the world's most powerful legislative bodies. There are a good many conditions that are inimical to presidential domination of Congress. Congress may adopt what the President proposes, but in the process change its accent and scope. Sometimes it merely disposes of what he proposes. Nothing in the President's plans is inviolable. No certainty exists that Congress will share his perceptions or succumb to his influence. The careers of individual legislators are not tightly linked to the President's, except perhaps in the case of those congressmen from marginal districts, and even here the link is firm only when the President's popularity is high. Indeed, some members of Congress have made their careers more secure through the visibility that comes from opposing the President and his program. Notwithstanding the world-wide trend toward executive supremacy, Congress remains a remarkably independent institution—a legislature almost as likely to resist executive initiatives as to embrace them.

---

[19] James Sundquist, *Politics and Policy: The Eisenhower, Kennedy, and Johnson Years* (Washington, D.C.: The Brookings Institution, 1968), pp. 478–479.

The President and Congress get along as well as they do because of one element which the President and some members of Congress have in common: party affiliation. In substantial measure party provides a frame of reference, an ideological underpinning, a rallying symbol, a structure for voting, and a language for testing and discussing ideas and policies. The congressman's constituency has never been the only valid criterion for assessing the wisdom of public policies. Congressmen prefer to ride along with their party if it is at all possible, if the costs do not loom too large. Moreover, the President and his legislative leaders are not at liberty to strike out in any direction they feel may be immediately popular with the voters. They are constrained by party platforms, by previous policy commitments, by interest group involvement, and by the need to consult with party officials and members at all levels, particularly with those who compose the congressional wing. Consensus politics is the essence of party processes.

President and Legislative Leaders   A recent study of majority party leadership in Congress indicates that a variety of alternatives are open to the President and party leaders in Congress in structuring their relations with one another. Typically, when the President and the majority leadership in Congress are of the same party, and the President assumes the role of "chief legislator," relations between the two branches have been characterized by cooperation. Within this pattern leaders tend to see themselves as lieutenants of the President, of necessity sensitive to his initiatives and responsible for his program. On the other hand, even though his party controls Congress, the President may decline to play a central role in the legislative process. In this situation, relations between the President and congressional leaders tend to be mixed and nonsupportive. Collegial rather than centralized leadership usually emerges as Congress generates its own legislative program instead of relying on presidential initiative. Finally, when the President and the majority in Congress (at least in one house) are of opposing parties (a so-called truncated majority), relations between the President and congressional leaders are often characterized by conflict and opposition. Leadership tends to be highly centralized, but legislative successes are usually few in number. "The leader of a truncated majority has great room for maneuver in the tactics of opposition and embarrassment on the domestic front, if his followers are willing to go along with him, but he must necessarily remain partially frustrated by his inability to accomplish much of his program domestically."[20]

David Truman has described the relationship between the President and

[20] From Randall B. Ripley, *Majority Party Leadership in Congress*, p. 175. Copyright © 1969, Little, Brown and Company, Inc. Reprinted by permission.

the elective leaders of his congressional party as one of "functional inter-dependence." There are mutual advantages in this interdependence. The President needs information in order to make intelligent judgments, and the leaders can supply it. Moreover, they can offer him policy guidance. At the same time, the leaders can do their jobs better if bolstered by the initiatives and leverage of the President. They have no power to give orders. They can only bargain and negotiate, and their effectiveness in doing this, in notable measure, is tied to the President's prestige and political assets. The nature of their jobs makes it important for the President's program to move through Congress. If he wins, they win; if he loses, they lose.[21]

The Role of the Minority Party in Congress   A recent study by Charles O. Jones identifies a number of political conditions that individually and in combination help to shape the role that the minority party plays in mobilizing congressional majorities and in shaping public policy. Some of these conditions originate outside Congress while others manifest themselves inside Congress. The principal external forces are the temper of the times (for example, the presence of a domestic or international crisis), the relative political strength of the minority party in the electorate, the degree of unity within the parties outside Congress, and the power of the President and his willingness to use the advantages that are inherent in his office. Conditions within Congress that affect minority party behavior are legislative procedures, the majority party's margin over the minority, the relative effectiveness of majority and minority party leadership, the length of time of the party in a minority status (perhaps contributing to a "minority party mentality"), and the relative strength of the party in the other house.[22]

The important point to recognize about the behavior of the minority party is that the strategies open to it are determined not simply by the preferences of the leadership or the rank-and-file members, by idiosyncratic circumstances, or by opportunities thrust up from time to time. Rather, what it does is influenced to a significant extent by conditions of varying importance over which it has little or no control. By and large, the conditions most likely to affect the minority party's behavior and shape its strategies are, among the external group, party unity and presidential power, and among the internal group, the size of the margin and the effectiveness of party leaders in both parties. Although restrictive political conditions depress the range of alternatives available to the minority party, a resourceful minority leadership can occasionally overcome them, enabling the minority party

---

[21] See Truman, *The Congressional Party*, especially pp. 279–319.
[22] Charles O. Jones, *The Minority Party in Congress* (Boston: Little, Brown, 1970), especially pp. 9–24.

to assume an aggressive, creative role in the legislative process. Among twentieth-century Congresses, however, this has been the exception, not the rule.[23]

The Party in Congress

It is about as difficult to write about congressional parties without revealing ambivalence as it is to pin a butterfly without first netting it. The party is hard to catch in a light that discloses all its qualities or its basic significance. Party is the organizing mechanism of Congress, and Congress could not do without it. It is hard to imagine how Congress could assemble itself for work, process the claims made upon it, lend itself to majority coalition-building, or be held accountable in any fashion without a wide range of party activities in its midst. Moreover, there are some sessions of Congress in which the only way to understand what Congress has done is to focus heavily on the performance of the majority party. But that is only part of the story. In the critical area of policy formation, majority party control often slips away, to be replaced by enduring biparty alliances or coalitions of expediency. Party counts, in other words, but not altogether predictably— hence the reason for the ambivalence in assessing the role of the congressional party.

Summary arguments may help to establish a perspective in the analysis. The indifferent success that sometimes characterizes party efforts in Congress, in fact, is not hard to explain. The odds are stacked against the party. In the first place, members of Congress are elected under a variety of conditions in a variety of constituencies: they are elected in environments where local party organizations are powerful and where they are weak; where populations are homogeneous and where they are heterogeneous; where competition is intense and where it is absent; where the level of voter education is relatively high and where it is relatively low; where income is relatively high and where it is relatively low; and where one or a few interests are dominant and where a multiplicity of interests compete for the advantages government can confer. The mix within congressional parties is a product of the mix within the nation's constituencies. It could scarcely be otherwise. The net result of diversity is that the men and women who make their way to Con-

---

[23] This study identifies eight strategies open to the minority party in the overall task of building majorities in Congress: support of the majority party by contributing votes and possibly leadership, inconsequential opposition, withdrawal, cooperation, innovation, consequential partisan opposition, consequential constructive opposition, and participation (the last strategy representing a situation in which the minority party controls the White House and thus is required to participate in constructing majorities). Strategies may vary within a single session of Congress and from one stage of the legislative process to the next. Jones, *The Minority Party in Congress*, pp. 19–24 and Chapters 4–8.

"So far, my mail is running three to one in favor of my position."

Drawing by Robt. Day; © 1970 The New Yorker Magazine, Inc.

gress see the world in different ways, stress different values, and pursue different objectives. A vast amount of disagreement inevitably lurks behind each party's label.

In the second place, the salient fact in the life of the legislator is his career. If he fails to protect it, no one else will. The congressman knows that his party can do very little to enhance his security in office or, conversely, very little to threaten it. The truth of the matter is that the congressman is on his own. Whether he is reelected or not will depend more on the decisions he makes than on those his party makes, more on how he "cultivates" his constituency than on how the party "cultivates" the nation. A sweeping electoral tide may, of course, carry him out of office; though this is to be feared from time to time, there is not much he can do about it. Hence the typical congressman concentrates on immediate problems. He takes his constituency as it is; if he monitors and defends its interests carefully he stands a good chance of having a long career in Congress, no matter what fate deals to his party.

Third, party efforts are confounded by the fragmentation of power within Congress. The seniority leaders who chair the major committees are as likely to have keys to congressional power as the elected party leaders.[24] Committees go their separate ways, sometimes in harmony with the party leadership and sometimes not. Powerful committees, such as the House Rules Committee, are sometimes under the control of party elements that are out of step with the leadership and with national party goals. No power to command rests with the party leadership, and there is not a great deal it can do to bring into line those members who steadily defy the party and thwart its objectives. The party caucus (or conference) is far from powerful, and the policy committees have never in any real sense functioned as policy-shaping agencies. "Parties" within parties, such as the House Democratic Study Group, bear witness to the lack of party agreement on public policy.

Fourth, the very nature of the legislative process makes it difficult for the parties to function smoothly. For the party to maintain firm control, it must create majorities at a number of stages in the legislative process: first in the standing committee, then on the floor, and last in the conference committee. In the House of Representatives a majority will also be needed in the Rules Committee. Failure to achieve a majority at any stage is likely to mean the loss of legislation. Even those bills that pass through the "obstacle course" may be so sharply changed as to be scarcely recognizable by their sponsors. In contrast, the opponents of legislation have only one requirement: to splice together a majority at one stage in the decision-making process. Breaking the party leadership at some point in the chain requires neither great resources nor imagination. For these reasons the adoption of a new public policy is immeasurably more difficult than the preservation of an old one. All the advantages, it seems, rest with those legislators bent on preserving existing arrangements.

Finally, the congressional party functions as it does because, by and large, it is a microcosm of the party in the electorate, beset by the same internal conflicts. The American political party is an extraordinary collection of diverse, conflicting interests and individuals brought together for the specific

[24] At the opening of the 92nd Congress (1971), both the House Democrats and Republicans altered somewhat their rules on the seniority system. Under the new Democratic rule, any ten members can demand a caucus vote on the retention of the chairman of any committee. An early attempt to remove the chairman of the District of Columbia Committee, a southerner who had chaired the committee for over twenty years, failed in the Democratic caucus by a margin of thirty votes. The new seniority rule of the House Republicans provides that the nominations made by the party's committee on committees for chairman or ranking member shall be subject to a secret vote in the Republican conference (caucus). The long-run impact of these changes in party rules is problematical. Although it is unlikely that many chairmen or ranking members will be deposed under either party's rules, these leaders may become more sensitive to the interests of committee members and the elected party leadership, knowing that the option is available.

purpose of winning office. The coalition carefully put together in order to make a bid for power comes under heavy stress once the election is over and candidates have become officeholders. Differences ignored or minimized during the campaign soon come to the surface. Party claims become only one input among many the congressman considers in shaping his positions on policy questions. Not surprisingly, for reasons already noted, national party objectives may be disregarded as the congressman sorts out his own priorities and takes account of those interests, including his local party organization, whose support he deems essential to his election the next time around.

The astonishing fact about the congressional parties is that they perform as well as they do. One reason for this is the phenomenon of party loyalty— the typical member is more comfortable when he votes in league with his party colleagues than when he opposes them. Another reason is that most members within each party represent constituencies that are broadly comparable in makeup; in "voting their district" they are likely to be in harmony with the general thrust of their party.[25] A third reason is found in the informal powers of the elected leaders. Members who respond to their leadership may be given assistance in advancing their "pet" legislation, awarded with an appointment to a prestigious committee, or armed with important information. There are advantages to "getting along" with the leadership. Lastly, there is a great deal of evidence that presidential leadership serves as a unifying force for his congressional party. Members may not go along with the President gladly, but many of them do go along, and even those who do not give his requests more than a second thought.

[25] The typical northern Democrat is elected from a district with these characteristics: higher proportion of nonwhite population, lower owner-occupancy of dwellings, higher population density, and higher percentage of urban population. The typical northern Republican represents a district whose characteristics are just the opposite. Constituency characteristics undoubtedly have an important impact on congressional voting. See Lewis A. Froman, Jr., "Inter-Party Constituency Differences and Congressional Voting Behavior," *American Political Science Review*, LVII (March 1963), pp. 57–61.

6

The American Party System:
Problems and Perspectives

ling the virtues of the American party system is something of an
in popular thought and scholarship. A few scholars, to be sure,
und substantial merit in the party system, particularly in its contri-
to unifying the nation, augmenting political stability, reconciling
onflict, and institutionalizing popular control of government. But the
hrust of commentary about this basic political institution has been
critical. American parties, a variety of indictments contend, are too
alike in their programs to afford voters a meaningful choice, are
ted by oligarchs or by organized special interests, are unable to deal
atively with national problems, are beset by a confusion of purposes,
ffective because of their internal divisions, are short on discipline and
on, are insufficiently responsive to popular claims, and are deficient as
ients for assuming and achieving responsibility in government.

The Doctrine of Responsible Parties

The major ground for popular distress over the parties may be simply
that most people are in some measure suspicious of politicians and their
organizations ("machines"). The criticism of scholars, on the other hand,
has focused mainly on the lack of party responsibility in government. The
most comprehensive statement on behalf of the doctrine of party responsibility
is found in a report of the Committee on Political Parties of the American
Political Science Association, *Toward a More Responsible Two-Party System*,
published in 1950. The report argues that what is required is a party
system that is "democratic, responsible, and effective." In the words of the
Committee:

> Party responsibility means the responsibility of both parties to the general
> public, as enforced in elections. Party responsibility to the public, enforced in
> elections, implies that there be more than one party, for the public can hold a
> party responsible only if it has a choice. . . . When the parties lack the capacity
> to define their actions in terms of policies, they turn irresponsible because the

131

electoral choice between the parties becomes devoid of meaning. . . . An effective party system requires, first, that the parties are able to bring forth programs to which they commit themselves and, second, that the parties possess sufficient internal cohesion to carry out these programs.[1]

Two major presumptions underlie the doctrine of responsible parties. The first is that the essence of democracy is to be found in popular control over government rather than in popular participation in the immediate tasks of government. A nation such as the United States is far too large and its government much too complex for the general run of citizens to become steadily involved in its decision-making processes. But this fact does not rule out popular control over government. The direction of government can be controlled by the people so long as they are consulted on public matters and possess the power to replace one set of rulers with another set, the "opposition." The party, in this view, becomes the instrument through which the public—or more precisely, a majority of the public—can decide who will run the government and for what purposes. Government by responsible parties is thus an expression of majority rule.

The second tenet in this theory holds that popular control over government requires that the public be given a choice between competing, unified parties capable of assuming collective responsibility to the public for the actions of government. The contributions of a responsible party system would be three in number. One, it "would enable the people to choose effectively a general program, a general direction for government to take, as embodied in a set of leaders committed to that program." Two, it would help to "energize and activate" public opinion. Three, it would increase the prospects for popular control by substituting the collective responsibility of an organized group, the party, for the individual responsibility assumed, more or less inadequately, by individual officeholders.[2]

If a responsible party system is held to be a desirable goal, what changes in party structures and processes might help to achieve it? The recommendations of the Committee on Political Parties of the American Political Science Association are worth considering. Designed to free the parties from traditional restraints and deficiencies, the Committee's principal proposals are concerned with the restructuring of the national party organization, party platforms, congressional party organization, intraparty democracy, and nominations and elections.

[1] All of the proposals for reforming the party system cited in this section, along with quoted material, are drawn from the report, *Toward a More Responsible Two-Party System* (New York: Holt, Rinehart and Winston, 1950). The longer quotations appear on these pages of the report: definition of party responsibility (pp. 1, 2, 22); seniority (pp. 61–62); intraparty democracy (p. 66); and party membership (pp. 69–70).

[2] For a comprehensive development of the themes of this and the previous paragraph, see Austin Ranney, *The Doctrine of Responsible Party Government* (Urbana: University of Illinois Press, 1954), pp. 10–16.

National Party Organization   The national party organizations envisaged by the Committee would be sharply different from those that exist today. The national convention, for example, would be composed of not more than 500 to 600 members, over half of whom would be elected by party voters. Ex officio members drawn from the ranks of the national committee, state party chairmen, and congressional leaders, along with certain prominent party leaders outside the party organizations, would make up the balance of the convention membership. Instead of meeting every four years, the convention would assemble regularly at least once every two years and perhaps in special meetings. Reduced in size, more representative of the actual strength of the party in individual states, and meeting more frequently and for longer periods, the "new" convention would gain effectiveness as a deliberative body for the development of party policy and as a more representative assembly for reconciling the interests of various elements within the party.

The most far-reaching proposal for restructuring national party organization calls for the creation of a party council of perhaps fifty members, composed of representatives from such units as the national committee, the congressional parties, the state committees, and the party's governors. Meeting regularly and often, the policy council would examine problems of party management, prepare a preliminary draft of the party platform for submission to the national convention, interpret the platform adopted by the convention, screen and recommend candidates for congressional offices, consider possible presidential candidates, and advise such appropriate party organs as the national convention or national committee "with respect to conspicuous departures from general party decisions by state or local party organizations." Empowered in this fashion, the party council would represent a firm break with familiar and conventional arrangements that contribute to the dispersion of party authority and the elusiveness of party policy. The essence of the council's task would be to blend the interests of national, congressional, and state organizations in such a way as to foster the development of an authentic national party, one capable of fashioning and implementing coherent strategies and policies.

Party Platforms   In the judgment of the Committee, party platforms are deficient on a number of counts. At times the platform "may be intentionally written in an ambiguous manner so as to attract voters of any persuasion and to offend as few voters as possible." State party platforms frequently espouse principles and policies in conflict with those of the national party. Congressional candidates and members of Congress may feel little obligation to support platform planks. No agency exists to interpret and apply the platform in the years between conventions. There is substantial confusion and difference of opinion over the binding quality of a platform—that is, whether party candidates are bound to observe the commitments presumably made in the adoption of the platform. Such are the principal shortcomings of this instrumentality.

To put new life back into the party platform, the Committee recommends that it should be written at least every two years in order to take account of developing issues and to link it to congressional campaigns in off-year elections; that it should "emphasize general party principles and national issues" which "should be regarded as binding commitments on all candidates and officeholders of the party, national, state and local"; that state and local platforms "should be expected to conform to the national platform on matters of general party principle or on national policies"; and that the party council should take an active role in the platform-making process, both in preparing tentative drafts of the document in advance of the convention and in interpreting and applying the platform between conventions. In sum, the Committee's argument is that party platforms and the processes through which they are presently formulated and implemented are inimical to the development of strong and responsible parties.

Congressional Party Organization   One of the most vexing problems in the effort to develop more responsible parties has been the performance of the congressional parties. The proliferation of leadership committees in Congress, the weakness of the caucus (or conference), the independence of congressional committees, and the seniority system have combined to limit possibilities for the parties to develop consistent and coherent legislative records. To tighten up congressional party organization, the Committee makes five comprehensive recommendations. First, each party in both the Senate and the House should consolidate its various leadership groups (for example, policy committees, steering committees, committees on committees, House Rules Committee) into a single leadership group; its functions would be to manage legislative party affairs, submit policy proposals to the membership, draw up slates of committee assignments, and assume responsibility for scheduling legislation.

Second, there should be more frequent meetings of the party caucuses, their decisions to be binding on legislation involving the party's principles and programs. Moreover, members of Congress who ignore a caucus decision "should not expect to receive the same consideration in the assignment of committee posts or in the apportionment of patronage as those who have been loyal to party principles."

Third, the seniority system should be made to work in harmony with the party's responsibility for a legislative program. In the words of the Committee:

The problem is not one of abolishing seniority and then finding an alternative. It is one of mobilizing the power through which the party leadership can successfully use the seniority principle rather than have the seniority principle dominate Congress. . . . Advancement within a committee on the basis of seniority makes sense, other things being equal. But it is not playing the game fairly for party members who oppose the commitments in their party's platform to rely on seniority to carry them into committee chairmanships. Party leaders have compelling reason to prevent such a member from becoming chairman— and they are entirely free so to exert their influence.

Fourth, the assignment of members of Congress to committees should be a responsibility of the party leadership committees. "Personal competence and party loyalty should be valued more highly than seniority in assigning members to such major committees as those dealing with fiscal policy and foreign affairs." At the same time, committee assignments should be reviewed at least every two years by the party caucus. A greater measure of party control over committee assignments is essential, if the party is to assume responsibility for a legislative program.

Finally, party leaders should take over the function of scheduling legislation for floor consideration. In particular, the power held by the House Rules Committee over legislative scheduling should be vested in the party leadership committee. If the party cannot control the flow of legislation to the floor and shape the agenda, there is little chance that it can control legislative output, which is the essence of responsible party performance in Congress.

Intraparty Democracy   The achievement of a system of responsible parties demands more than the good intentions of the public and of party leaders. It requires widespread and meaningful political participation by grass-roots members of the party, democratic party processes, and an accountable leadership. The Committee observes:

> Capacity for internal agreement, democratically arrived at, is a critical test for a party. It is a critical test because when there is no such capacity, there is no capacity for positive action, and hence the party becomes a hollow pretense. It is a test which can be met only if the party machinery affords the membership an opportunity to set the course of the party and to control those who speak for it. This test can be met fully only where the membership accepts responsibility for creative participation in shaping the party's program.

There is, of course, nothing easy about the task of developing an active party membership capable of creative participation in the affairs of the party. Organizational changes at both the summit and the base of the party hierarchy are required. "A national convention, broadly and directly representative of the rank and file of the party and meeting at least biennially, is essential to promote a sense of identity with the party throughout the membership as well as to settle internal differences fairly, harmoniously, and democratically." Similarly, at the grass-roots level, there is need for the development of local party groups that will meet frequently to generate and discuss ideas concerning national issues and the national party program. The emergence and development of local, issue-oriented party groups can be facilitated by national party agencies engaged in education and publicity and willing to undertake the function of disseminating information and research findings.

A new concept of party membership is required—one that emphasizes "allegiance to a common program" rather than mere support of party candidates in elections. The Committee suggests that its development might take this form:

> The existence of a national program, drafted at frequent intervals by a party convention both broadly representative and enjoying prestige, should make a great difference. It would prompt those who identify themselves as Republicans and Democrats to think in terms of support of that program, rather than in terms of personalities, patronage, and local matters. . . . Once machinery is established which gives the party member and his representative a share in framing the party's objectives, once there are safeguards against internal dictation by a few in positions of influence, members and representatives will feel readier to assume an obligation to support the program. Membership defined in these terms does not ask for mindless discipline enforced from above. It generates the self-discipline which stems from free identification with aims one helps to define.

Nominations and Elections   The Committee's recommendations for changing nomination and election procedures fit comfortably within its overall political formula for strengthening the American party system. It endorses the direct primary—"a useful weapon in the arsenal of intraparty democracy"—while expressing preference for the *closed* rather than the open version. The open primary is inconsistent with the idea of a responsible party system, since by permitting voters to shift from one party to the other between primaries, it subverts the concept of membership as the foundation of party organization. The Committee also supports the use of preprimary meetings of party committees for the purpose of proposing and endorsing candidates in primary elections. Selection of delegates to the national conventions should be made by the direct vote of party members rather than by state conventions. Local party groups should meet prior to the convention in order to discuss potential candidates and platform planks.

The Committee also recommends that three major changes should be made in the election system. The electoral college should be changed in order to give "all sections of the country a real voice in electing the President and the Vice-President" and to help develop a two-party system in areas now dominated by one party. And second, the term of members of the House of Representatives should be extended from two to four years, with coinciding election of House members and the President. Were this constitutional change to be made, prospects would be improved for harmonizing executive and legislative power through the agency of party. Finally, the Committee supports a variety of changes in the regulation of campaign finance, the most important of which calls for a measure of government support to be used in meeting the campaign costs of the parties.

The Committee Report: An Overview

In the broadest sense, the publication of the report, *Toward a More Responsible Two-Party System,* was an outgrowth of the growing uneasiness among many political scientists over the performance of the nation's party system and the vitality of American government. Specifically, the report sought to come to terms with a problem that is central to the overall political system: the weakness of political parties as instruments for governing in a democratic and responsible fashion. The report is not a study in political feasibility. It does not offer a blueprint depicting where the best opportunities lie for making changes in the party system. What it does offer is a set of wide-ranging prescriptions consonant with a particular model of political organization. If the model sketched by the Committee were to come into existence, the American party system would bear only modest resemblance to that which has survived for well over a century. The key characteristics of the new parties would be the national quality of their organization, a much greater degree of centralization of party power, a tendency for party claims to assume primacy over individual constituency claims in public policy formation, a heightened visibility for the congressional parties and their leadership, and for the President's role as party leader, and a greater concern over party unity and discipline.

To its credit, the report was not accompanied by the usual somnolence that settles over prescriptive efforts of this kind. Nor, on the other hand, did queues of reformers form in the streets, in the universities, or elsewhere to push for its implementation. What happened rather is that the report gave substantial impetus to the study of American political parties and helped to foster a concern for reform that, in one respect or another, continues to the present.[3]

---

[3] To explore recent literature which considers the reform of political parties and other basic political institutions affected by the parties, see James MacGregor Burns,

The APSA report is the most comprehensive case for reform of the party system yet produced. Nonetheless, in the judgment of certain critics, the report suffers from a number of flaws. Four principal criticisms have been lodged against it:

1. *The existing party system is not as irresponsible as the Committee portrays it.* In judging party platforms, the Committee argues that "alternatives between the parties are defined so badly that it is often difficult to determine what the election has decided even in the broadest terms." Yet a careful comparison of party platforms, the argument runs, will reveal important differences between the parties in such issue areas as labor-management relations, taxes, and benefits for a variety of specific groups. Moreover, not only do the parties differ in their platforms, but the majority party ordinarily carries out most of the program set forth in its platform. In similar fashion, the Committee underestimates the extent to which the parties differ on public policy questions in Congress. Contrary to the Committee's assessment, there have been substantial differences over the years in the orientations of the parties toward questions involving the tariff, regulation of business, national defense, foreign relations, civil rights, agricultural policy, social welfare legislation, and the allocation of power between the national government and state governments. The attentive voter, according to this view, should have little difficulty in distinguishing the broad commitments of each party in Congress.[4]

2. *The responsible parties model is fundamentally incompatible with exist-*

The Deadlock of Democracy (Englewood Cliffs, N.J.: Prentice-Hall, 1963); Stephen K. Bailey, *The Condition of Our National Political Parties* (New York: Fund for the Republic, 1959) and *Congress in the Seventies* (New York: St. Martin's Press, 1970); Marian D. Irish (ed.), *The Continuing Crisis in American Politics* (Englewood Cliffs, N.J.: Prentice-Hall, 1963); Robert Bendiner, *Obstacle Course on Capitol Hill* (New York: McGraw-Hill, 1965); Daniel M. Berman, *In Congress Assembled* (New York: Macmillan, 1964); Lewis A. Froman, *The Congressional Process* (Boston: Little, Brown, 1967), especially Chapters 10 and 11; and John S. Saloma III, *Congress and the New Politics* (Boston: Little, Brown, 1969), especially Chapter 8. Of special interest, see two recent papers directed specifically to the report, *Toward a More Responsible Two-Party System*: Evron M. Kirkpatrick, "Toward a More Responsible Two-Party System: Political Science, Policy Science, or Pseudo-Science?," and Gerald M. Pomper, "After Twenty Years: The Report of the APSA Committee on Political Parties," both delivered at the Annual Meeting of the American Political Science Association, Los Angeles, September 8–12, 1970.

[4] The general line of argument developed in this paragraph is derived from Julius Turner, "Responsible Parties: A Dissent from the Floor," *American Political Science Review*, XLV (March 1951), pp. 143–152; quotation on p. 145. For a recent study of the differences between the parties (1944–1964) in the content of their platforms and in voting on platform proposals in Congress, see Gerald M. Pomper, *Elections in America: Control and Influence in Democratic Politics* (New York: Dodd, Mead, 1968), pp. 192–203. Pomper finds that significant differences between the parties occur on about a tenth of all platform planks. A very high proportion of these platform conflicts later produce conflict between the parties in Congress—89 percent during the Truman Administration and 87 percent in both the Eisenhower and Kennedy Administrations.

ing constitutional arrangements and with contemporary political culture. The position of the Committee is that "the weakness of the American two-party system can be overcome as soon as a substantial part of the electorate wants it overcome." In counterpoise, many scholars believe that the form that political parties have taken in the United States is due in large part to the character of the political system itself. Moreover, the parties not only have become accustomed to functioning within the constraints presented by the political system but in fact help to make it work and preserve it. Federalism, the separation of powers, checks and balances, staggered terms of office, independence of the judiciary, and a political culture that stresses minority rights fully as much as majority rule—all are critical elements in the "total system of anti-majoritarian government" established by the Founding Fathers. Given the obstacles that this "total system" presents, a highly centralized party system—one capable of assuming generalized control over the whole of government—is not only unlikely to be achieved but also is inappropriate to the political environment. Finally, there is no evidence to indicate that the public at large either understands or prefers a party system of such an order—one that, by its very nature, would be built on the doctrine of majority-rule democracy.[5]

3. *The voting behavior and attitudes of the American people would have to change markedly in order to accommodate to the model of centralized parties.* The problem of gaining support for comprehensive party reform may not be so much a matter of winning politicians to its side—difficult as that may be—as it is to educate the voters to its virtues and to bring their voting habits into harmony with a new concept of party. Many voters are more oriented to candidates than they are to parties or issues. Is there any reason to believe that the public would prefer elections in which the critical question is the parties' programs rather than the personal characteristics of the candidates?[6] Are the voters able to distinguish between the parties in programmatic terms? For the present, except for a relatively small proportion of people, the answers to these questions appear to be no. The results of a vari-

[5] For further exposition of the incompatibility argument, see Austin Ranney, "Toward a More Responsible Two-Party System: A Commentary," *American Political Science Review*, XLV (June 1951), pp. 488–499; quotation on p. 497. Implicit in the Committee report, Murray S. Stedman and Herbert Sonthoff contend, is the assumption that "majority rule is preferable to consensus rule, and that anything less than majority rule is, in a technical sense, irresponsible." The Committee fails to explain why rule by compromise is "less efficacious and less democratic than rule by one party, even though it be the majority party." Furthermore, "majority rule in its strict, arithmetical sense refers to the degree rather than to the mode of agreement. It means merely opposition to the idea of minority rule, and needs by no means to be considered, therefore, as an alternative to the rule by consensus." See Murray S. Stedman and Herbert Sonthoff, "Party Responsibility—A Critical Inquiry," *Western Political Quarterly*, IV (September 1951), pp. 454–468; quotations on pp. 454–455.

[6] On the matter of public support for the idea of responsible party government, see the evidence in Chapter 1, pp. 6–9.

ety of recent studies show that generalized ideological concerns are held by only a small proportion of the American people. In the 1956 presidential election, for example, only 15 percent of the voters were able to evaluate the candidates and the parties in terms reflecting a capacity to make ideological distinctions; a mere 3.5 percent, in fact, held conceptions of politics sufficiently well developed and integrated to be classified as "ideologues."[7] Studies of the 1960 and 1964 elections, furthermore, reveal that for about one-half of the electorate the terms "liberal" and "conservative" carry no meaning what-soever.[8] The indifference of the public to the idea of programmatic parties would appear to represent a major obstacle to rationalizing the party system along the lines of the responsible parties model.[9]

Not only would a responsible party system require changes in the voting habits and attitudes of the public but it would also necessitate changes in the relationship between constituents and their representatives. The constituencies, for example, are remarkably diverse; public policy that is advantageous to constituencies of one kind may not satisfy the interests of constituencies of another kind. Legislators long accustomed to the role of defending and pro-moting specific constituency interests would undoubtedly find it difficult to submerge parochial concerns in favor of party claims. In the second place, it seems likely that a responsible party system would alter in some measure the constituent-representative relationship in matters involving the individual problems of citizens. As it is, members of Congress devote an extraordinary amount of time and energy to finding solutions to the special problems of

---

[7] Angus Campbell, et al., The American Voter, p. 249.

[8] Philip E. Converse, "The Nature of Belief Systems in Mass Publics," in David E. Apter (ed.), Ideology and Discontent (London: The Free Press, 1964), p. 222; and Philip E. Converse, Aage Clausen, and Warren E. Miller, "Electoral Myth and Reality: The 1964 Election," American Political Science Review, LIX (June 1965), p. 335. There is considerable irony in the fact that ideology held such slight significance for voters in 1964, an election which was expected to produce a sharp ideological clash between the conservatism of Barry Goldwater and the liberalism of Lyndon Johnson. Most voters, however, failed to perceive the election in ideological terms. Political ideology, it seems, simply lacks salience for the typical voter.

[9] Contrary to the broad thrust of this paragraph, there is some recent evidence of a growing correspondence between party identification and policy orientation in the elec-torate. A comparison of national voter samples in 1956 and 1968 by Gerald Pomper shows that on a number of major policy issues—for example, federal aid to education, government provision of medical care, government guarantee of full employment, and federal enforcement of fair employment and fair housing—the differences between Democratic and Republican voters have become substantially greater. The 1968 survey shows that Democratic and Republican partisans clearly differ in their support for these policies—that is, the Democrats much more likely to take the "liberal" position of sup-port for governmental action. Moreover, the proportion of voters who are able to perceive differences between the parties on these policy questions was significantly larger in 1968 than in 1956. "Whatever the causes," writes Pomper, "the electorate now more fully satisfies one of the basic conditions for a responsible party system. It is beginning to perceive party differences and to be agreed on the differing positions of the parties." Pomper "After Twenty Years: The Report of the APSA Committee on Political Parties."

constituents that arise from the fact that government touches their lives in countless ways. "Errand running" for "the folks back home" is an important activity for all congressmen, a preoccupation for some congressmen and in the lore of politics, the *sine qua non* for reelection. Whether this role of "Washington Representative" would be fully compatible with centralized, programmatic parties is at least open to doubt.

4. *The price for the development of a centralized party system may be more than the American people are willing to pay.* Major change in the party system, it has been argued frequently, cannot be brought about without setting in motion certain forces that would alter the character of the political system as a whole. Among the consequences that might ensue, according to one line of analysis, are the breakdown of federalism, the emergence of a multiple party system, and the loss of consensus.[10]

The principal aim of the proponents of party responsibility is to centralize power in the national parties. Some measure of the independence of state and local parties would undoubtedly be lost in the process of strengthening the national party apparatus. Ranney and Kendall observe:

> The technique for [achieving centralized parties] is to vest control of the state and local parties—and, through them, the state and local governments—in the hands of national party leaders, so that state and local interference with national programs will be reduced to an absolute minimum. It may well be, therefore, that if such a party system were developed in the United States, it would mean the end of the reality if not of the form of federalism, and the states would become little more than administrative subdivisions of the national government.[11]

A second possibility is that the development of centralized and disciplined parties might contribute to the formation of "splinter" parties and eventually to a full-blown multiple-party system. Although the factors that undergird the two-party system are not fully understood, it seems evident that one of its principal supports is the persistent inclination of each party to appeal to a broad band of interests. Each major party holds some attractiveness for all elements of the electorate. Virtually no interest—at least no organized interest—is too small to be ignored by the leaders of either party. Moreover, party leaders themselves represent a variety of different interests. In a word, diversity abounds in the major parties. The key question is whether two disciplined national parties, each distinguished by a fairly rigorous and consistent program, could continue to be hospitable to a wide range of interests. If one party were to become the domain of "liberals" and the other party the home

[10] See Ranney and Kendall, *Democracy and the American Party System*, (New York: Harcourt Brace Jovanovich, Inc., 1956), pp. 530–532. Their analysis forms the basis for this discussion. See also T. William Goodman, "How Much Political Party Centralization Do We Want?" *Journal of Politics*, XIII (November 1951), pp. 536–561, and Turner, "Responsible Parties: A Dissent from the Floor," pp. 149–152.

[11] Ranney and Kendall, *Democracy and the American Party System*, p. 530.

of "conservatives," as seems the likely development, could all groups fit comfortably within such a party structure? It is a good guess, say critics, that some groups (for example, economic, sectional, or local) would resist lodgment in either party. Despite the obstacles to the launching of a new party, such efforts likely would be made by those elements unable to gain satisfaction from the major parties. Eventually, a multiple-party system might result.

Finally, there is a possibility that a new party system would have a pernicious effect on the maintenance of consensus within the nation. Almost certainly the "reformed" parties would present markedly different appeals to the electorate. The range of ambiguity within party programs would be narrowed. Voters and groups alike would find it necessary to choose sides. Ultimately, group would be positioned against group and class against class. Never far below the surface in any case, conflict would intensify as the stakes between winning and losing increased in visibility and importance. Were this to be the script followed, the price paid by the American people would be the disintegration of consensus.

The goal of advocates of party responsibility is to place the parties at the creative center of policy-making in the United States. That is what party responsibility is all about. Voters would choose between two disciplined and cohesive parties, each distinguished by relatively clear and consistent programs and policy orientations. Responsibility would be enforced through elections. Parties would be retained in power or removed from power in terms of their performance and the attractiveness of their programs. Collective responsibility for the conduct of government would displace the individual responsibility of officeholders. Such are the key characteristics of the model party system discussed in these pages.

Whether a more responsible two-party system would be accompanied by the consequences critics have forecast is impossible to say. There is plainly some risk that disciplined parties might contribute to an erosion of consensus, to heightened conflict between classes, and even to an infusion of splinter parties created by elements finding the major parties unresponsive to their needs. But there is no certainty that these consequences would ensue. The broad fact is that despite this country's long experience with a two-party system, there is much yet to be known about it. Extracting it, for purposes of analysis, from the political system as a whole is difficult at best. Moreover, the American political system, like the society in which it functions, is an entity of extraordinary complexity. Constitutional arrangements, traditions, conventions, and the beliefs and values of the public and its leaders all contribute in some measure to the shape, purposes, and stability of the political system and its institutions. That change in the American political system would result from the impact of disciplined parties is scarcely arguable. The line of change that would evolve, however, is anything but clear.

The more immediate and relevant question concerns the prospects for the development of strengthened parties in the United States—parties that resemble, in one degree or another, the responsible parties model. One can begin an answer to this question by examining the principal trends now notable in American politics.

Trends in American Politics

The outward signs of the vitality of American parties are perhaps illusory. It is true, of course, that the two major parties continue to dominate office-holding in the United States. The vast majority of aspirants for public office carry on their campaigns under the banner of one or the other of the two major parties. The most important fact to be known about the candidates in a great many electoral jurisdictions throughout the country is the party to which they belong, so decisive is party orientation for election outcomes. Virtually everywhere, save in nonpartisan environments, the trappings of party— symbols, sponsorship, slogans, buttons, and literature—are as much in evidence today as ever in the past. The parties collect money, spend money, and incur campaign deficits on a scale that dwarfs their budgets of a generation ago. Party bureaucracies and party headquarters have never been larger or more fully staffed than they are today. Nearly three out of four citizens continue to see themselves as Democrats or Republicans, however imperfectly they may comprehend their party's program or the performance of their party's representatives. The number of auxiliary campaign groups in major elections almost defies enumeration; any person can find a way to contribute to the party cause through participation in the campaign activities of "citizen" and "volunteer" organizations. The aura of extravagance that surrounds national conventions gives scarcely a hint that the parties are in any way in trouble. And so it goes. Viewed at some distance, the American two-party system appears to be the picture of health. Whether this assessment is accurate can be better judged by examining changes that have occurred and are occurring in the party system and in the electorate.

1. *The loss of power by electoral party organizations.* At virtually every point associated with the recruitment and election of public officials, the party organizations have suffered an erosion of power. The reasons for this are many and varied. At the top of the list, perhaps, is the direct primary. "He who can make the nominations is the owner of the party," E. E. Schattschneider wrote some years ago, and there is no reason to doubt his observation.[12] In view of the fact that nonendorsed candidates may defeat party nominees in primaries, one may wonder whether, in some elections and in some jurisdictions, any one except the candidates really owns the parties.

---

[12] Schattschneider, *Party Government*, p. 64.

The party label has lost significance as candidates of all political colorations, with all variety of relationships to the organization, earn the right to wear it by capturing primary elections. Most important, a party that cannot control its nominations finds it difficult to achieve unity once it has won office and is faced with the implementation of its platform. Candidates who defeat the organization may see little reason to subscribe to party tenets, defend party interests, or follow party leaders. Not only does the primary contribute to the fragmentation of party unity in office but it also divides the party at large:

> Primaries often pit party leaders against party leaders, party voters against party voters, often opening deep and unhealing party wounds. They also dissipate party financial and personal resources. Party leadership usually finds that it has no choice but to take sides in a primary battle, the alternative being the possible triumph of the weaker candidate.[13]

Still other reasons may be adduced for the atrophy of the party's role in the electoral process. The great urban machines of a generation ago have all but disappeared in many places. Employing an intricate system of rewards and incentives, the machines dominated the political process—controlling access to power, political careers, and, most important, votes. Their decline, due to a number of reasons, has contributed to a growth of independence both within the electorate and among politicians. "Antiparty" appeals are sometimes as effective as working within the party to gain office. Defeated in the Republican primary in 1969, John V. Lindsay ran on the ticket of the Liberal party, formed an Independent party to secure another line on the ballot, and won the New York mayor's office in a convincing victory over his Democratic and Republican rivals. Broadly similar outcomes, occurring with increasing frequency, mark the politics of a number of other major cities. Party endorsement, it is evident, is less and less a guarantee of victory. In addition, the decline in the volume of patronage due to extension of the merit system, the decline in the attractiveness of patronage jobs in times of affluence, the steady growth of a better-educated electorate, the mobility of voters, the awesome costs of campaigns, the requirement for technical skills in the use of the mass media and in other innovative forms of campaigning, the emergence of the celebrity candidate, and the inability of the parties to capture the imagination and esteem of the voters—all contribute to an easing of the party grip on the processes by which individuals are recruited and elected to office.

2. *The decline of partisanship.* Although evidence for the argument must be assembled in bits and pieces (and also treated warily), there are several reasons to believe that a marked decline in partisanship has taken place in the American electorate. In the first place, there has been a notable growth in the proportion of voters who describe themselves as independents rather than as

---

[13] Frank J. Sorauf, *Political Parties in the American System*, p. 102. Copyright © 1964 Little, Brown and Company, Inc. Reprinted by permission.

partisans. Table 18 shows the political affiliation of a cross section of the general population and of the South in 1960 and 1970. According to the latter survey, 27 percent of the citizens are classified as independents. Especially interesting is the fact that the proportion of southerners regarding themselves as independents was much larger in 1970 than it was in 1960—27 percent as opposed to 19 percent.[14] Independence carries a particular attraction for younger voters. Among voters in the 21–29 age group, in a 1969 survey, 42 percent emerged as independents. College students are even more likely to be independents than the general run of younger voters: 52 percent of a nationwide sample surveyed in 1970 designated themselves as independents.[15] To be sure, not all the voters who perceive themselves as independents actually behave as independents; many doubtless are undercover partisans who stay with the same party election after election. Nonetheless, as the proportion of self-styled independents rises, problems mount for the maintenance of a vigorous party system. Voter independence is to party vitality what coalition legislative voting is to party responsibility—a relationship of conspicuous incompatibility.

Another thread of evidence that party linkage between voters and government has diminished may be found in the contrast between presidential votes in the nineteenth and twentieth centuries. In the sixteen presidential elections

Table 18
Political Affiliation in the Nation and in the South,
1960 and 1970*

	Democrat	*Republican*	*Independent*
National			
1960	47%	30%	23%
1970	44	29	27
South			
1960	59	22	19
1970	50	23	27

* The question asked was: "In politics, as of today, do you consider yourself a Republican, Democrat, or Independent?" Source: *Gallup Opinion Index*, Report No. 62, August 1970, p. 3 (as adapted).

[14] There is apparently a close relationship between the growth of independents in the South and the movement led by George Wallace. Over half of the persons who voted for Wallace in the 1968 presidential election classified themselves as independents in 1969. *Gallup Opinion Index*, Report No. 50, August 1969, p. 6.
[15] *Gallup Opinion Index*, Report No. 60, June 1970, p. 21. The striking number of young voters who now identify themselves as independents suggests that partisanship will continue to lose ground during the 1970s. Movement of 18-year-olds into the electorate will dramatically accentuate this trend. Thus the outlook for the next decade is for an increase in partisan volatility, due in significant degree simply to the "age table" of the country. See Philip E. Converse, "Change in the American Electorate," (Mimeograph, Survey Research Center, 1970), p. 91.

from 1836 to 1896, only the election of 1872 was of landslide dimensions—
that is, an election in which the winning candidate received at least 55 percent
of the two-party vote. By contrast, eight of the eighteen presidential elections
from 1900 through 1968 were decided by landslide margins. Movement across
party lines from election to election has become increasingly common.
Moreover, partisan swings have become substantially wider. To an important
extent, the party-oriented voter of the nineteenth century has been displaced
by the volatile voter of the twentieth century, resulting in a condition under
which contemporary party organizations are "at best only indifferently successful at mobilizing a stable, predictable mass base of support."[16]

The growth in the incidence of ticket-splitting also suggests a deterioration
in party ability to mobilize voters to cast a party vote—that is, to support the
entire ticket. The magnitude of ticket-splitting today is undoubtedly much

Table 19
Congressional Districts with Split Election Results:
Districts Carried by a Presidential Nominee of One
Party and by a House Nominee of Another Party,
1920–1968*

Year and Party of the Winning Presidential Candidate	*Number of Districts*	*Number of Districts With Split Results*	*Percent*
1920R	344	11	3.2
1924R	356	42	11.8
1928R	359	68	18.9
1932D	355	50	14.1
1936D	361	51	14.1
1940D	362	53	14.6
1944D	367	41	11.2
1948D	422	90	21.3
1952R	435	84	19.3
1956R	435	130	29.9
1960D	437	114	26.1
1964D	435	145	33.3
1968R	435	141	32.4
Total	5103	1020	19.9

* Source: Milton C. Cummings, Jr., *Congressmen and the Electorate* (New York: Free
Press, 1966), p. 32, as updated. Presidential returns for some congressional districts were not
available between 1920 and 1948.

[16] For further analysis of this theme, see Walter Dean Burnham, "The Changing
Shape of the American Political Universe," *American Political Science Review*, LIX
(March 1965), pp. 7–28. For the period 1872–1892, the mean national partisan swing
in presidential elections was 2.3 percent; for 1896–1916, 5 percent; for 1920–1932, 10.3
percent; and for 1936–1964, 5.4 percent. These data and the quotation are drawn from
pp. 22–23. See another article by Walter Dean Burnham, "The End of American Party
Politics," *Trans-Action*, VII (December 1969), pp. 12–22.

greater than it was a generation ago,[17] though its precise dimensions in different kinds of elections are unknown.[18] An important clue to this development may be found in an examination of the vote for presidential and congressional candidates within congressional districts. Table 19, the work of Milton Cummings, Jr., shows the number and percentage of congressional districts with split election results—districts won by the presidential candidate of one party and by the congressional candidate of another party—from 1920 to 1968.[19] It depicts a more or less steady increase in the number of split elections for these offices. A high point was reached in 1964 when one-third of all House districts split their results, doubtless due in great part to the Goldwater candidacy. It is interesting to note that there were more split election outcomes in the four elections between 1956 and 1968 than in the nine elections between 1920 and 1952.[20]

A phenomenon closely related to ticket-splitting is "party switching"—for example, voting for the presidential candidate of one party in one election and voting for the presidential candidate of another party the next election. Ordinarily, under two percent of the electorate will change its party identification in the period of a single year. Moreover, the net gain or loss to either major

[17] Scholars are agreed on this point, though comprehensive studies of ballot-splitting are in short supply. For example, Walter Dean Burnham writes: "The underlying partisan preferences of the electorate, as survey research has repeatedly demonstrated, have not significantly changed since at least the 1940s. But the electorate since 1950 has displayed a willingness to engage in ticket-splitting on an unprecedentedly massive scale. Probably as a consequence of image voting, the partial replacement of patronage politics by ideologically flavored politics, and the penetration of the mass media, short-term influences on voting have grown tremendously in recent years at the expense of long-term continuities." Water Dean Burnham, "Party Systems and the Political Process," in Chambers and Burnham (eds.), *The American Party Systems*, p. 304.

[18] A national sample of public opinion immediately following the 1968 presidential election disclosed that 54 percent of the voters had split their tickets (voted for candidates of different parties) as against 43 percent who had voted a straight ticket (with 3 percent in the "don't know" category). Split-ticket voting was particularly high among voters with these characteristics: college education (64 percent); professional, business, and white-collar occupations (62–63 percent); age group 21–29 (66 percent); self-styled independents (72 percent); and upper-income levels (60 percent). *Gallup Opinion Index*, Report No. 42, December 1968, p. 9.

[19] Milton Cummings, Jr., *Congressmen and the Electorate* (New York: Free Press, 1966); the extent and consequences of ticket-splitting are considered on pp. 28–55. The data of Table 19 provide only a partial view of the dimensions of ticket-splitting in contests for these offices. For example, substantial ticket-splitting nevertheless could be present even though the presidential candidate and the congressional candidate of the same party received total votes of the same size. The totals would be the same if, say, those voters who voted for the Republican presidential candidate and the House Democratic candidate were balanced by an equal number of voters who voted for the Democratic presidential candidate and the House Republican candidate.

[20] Another test of split-ticket voting is the spread, or difference, between the percentage of the vote received by the presidential and congressional candidates of the same party. Over the period 1920–1964, 30.8 percent of the districts had an election spread of under 2.5 percent, 49.1 percent of the districts under 5.0 percent, and 31.5

party is usually under one percent in a single year.[21] Such impressive stability can be misleading, for it is clear that, at times, citizens in far greater numbers abandon their parties at the polling place. Democrats by the millions deserted their party's presidential nominee in 1952, Adlai Stevenson, to vote for the Republican candidate, Dwight Eisenhower. Similarly, Republicans in droves cast their ballots for Lyndon Johnson in 1964 rather than Barry Goldwater, thus contributing substantially to the landslide Democratic vote. An even more massive switch took place in 1968. The Democratic proportion of the popular vote dropped by 19 percentage points, from over 61 percent to less than 43 percent. Forty percent of the votes received by Richard Nixon were cast by individuals who had voted for Lyndon Johnson in 1964.[22] Paradoxically, the Nixon victory occurred at a time when, according to voter surveys, two out of every three partisans professed allegiance to the Democratic party.

Finally, an ebbing of partisanship among the American people can be detected in a miscellany of public opinion surveys. For example, there is evidence that a large and increasing proportion of the population is inclined to report that:

(a) it doesn't make a great deal of difference which candidate wins the election or which party runs the country;

(b) whether the Democrats or Republicans win will not have an important impact on the financial positions of their families;

(c) they approve of the way the President is handling his job even though they are not members of the President's party; and

(d) there is no difference between the parties in their capacity to handle the

---

percent of the districts over 10 percent. The spread for recent elections notable for ticket-splitting may be contrasted:

Percentage of Districts in Which Vote Spread Was:*

	Under 2.5%	Under 5%	Over 10%
1920–1964	30.8%	49.1%	31.5%
1956	16.6	32.6	42.3
1960	22.0	40.7	37.1
1964	18.6	36.1	43.4

* These data are drawn from Cummings, *Congressmen and the Electorate*, p. 37.

[21] William H. Flanigan, *Political Behavior of the American Electorate* (Boston: Allyn and Bacon, 1968), p. 44.

[22] Philip E. Converse, Warren E. Miller, Jerrold G. Rusk, and Arthur G. Wolfe, "Continuity and Change in American Politics: Parties and Issues in the 1968 Election," *American Political Science Review*, LXIII (December 1969), p. 1084. Many of the voters in this group of 40 percent were, of course, Republicans returning to their party after their flight from Goldwater.

most important problems facing the country—for example, war, crime and lawlessness, race relations, inflation, poverty, and so on.[23]

The thrust of these attitudinal developments is that there is a growing consensus within the main body of American opinion. It is a product of the age of affluence, marked by increasing economic security among the working class and by growing acceptance of the welfare state by the middle class—so argues Robert E. Lane. Many of the cleavages that separated society in the past no longer carry the political and emotional impact they once did. Among the principal characteristics of a consensual politics is a growing belief that personal or group welfare will not be jeopardized by the victory of one party or the other. As a result, partisanship loses some of its "bite" and political decisions appear less threatening to national, personal, and group interests. The emerging pattern is one of "the interested, party-identified citizen, following politics at least as closely as he did in the days of the great intense clashes when the welfare state was first launched and when men were harassed by insecurity and poverty; voting more regularly, and, indeed 'personally caring' about the outcome as before; but believing that the national and personal stakes involved are not so great."[24]

3. *The growing importance of professional campaign management firms in politics.* American party organizations no longer dominate the process of winning political support for the candidates who run under their labels. This is one of the principal facts to be known about the party system today. The role of party organizations in campaigns has declined as professional management firms, pollsters, and media specialists—stirred by the prospects of new accounts and greater profits—have arrived on the political scene. Indeed, so important have they become in political campaigns, especially for major offices, that it often appears as if the party has been reduced to the role of spectator. To be sure, the parties continue to raise and spend money in large sums, to staff their headquarters with salaried personnel and volunteers, and to mobilize their precinct officials to turn out the vote on election day. What they do matters, of course, but much less so than in the past.

The center of major political campaigns now lies in the decisions and activities of individual candidates and in their use of consultants, campaign management firms, and the mass media—not in the party organizations or in the decisions of party leaders. Modern political campaigning calls for resources

[23] Trend data since the 1940s on points (a) to (c) appear in Robert E. Lane, "The Politics of Consensus in an Age of Affluence," *American Political Science Review*, LIX (December 1965), pp. 882–885. Concerning point (d), see issues of the *Gallup Opinion Index*, especially October 1965; September 1968; and February 1970. Typically, between 40 and 50 percent of the respondents report that they see no difference between the parties (or have no opinion) in this respect.

[24] Lane, "The Politics of Consensus in an Age of Affluence," p. 884.

and skills, which for the most part the party organization cannot furnish. Public opinion surveys are needed to pinpoint important issues, to locate sources of support and opposition, and to learn how voters appraise the qualities of the candidate. Electronic data processing is useful in the analysis of voting behavior and for the simulation of campaign decisions. For a fee the candidate with sufficient financial resources can avail himself of specialists of all kinds: public relations, advertising, fund-raising, communications, and financial counseling. He can hire experts in film-making, speech-writing, speech-coaching, voter registration, direct-mail letter campaigns, computer information services, time-buying (for radio and television), voter analysis, get-out-the-vote drives, and campaign strategy. Fewer and fewer things are left to chance or to the vicissitudes of party administration. What a candidate hears, says, does, wears, and possibly even thinks bears the heavy imprint of the specialist in campaign management.

There is, it seems, no end to the variety of services made available to candidates by management firms. The Campaign Communications Institute of America, Inc., has an arrangement under which a candidate low on cash can charge services on his American Express card. A glimpse of the other services CCI provides may be gained from this account:

> Under a middleman arrangement with some 35 manufacturing and service firms, [CCI] has produced a swollen bag of personalized vote-getting tricks. There are the routine items—bumper stickers, buttons, litter bags, matchbooks, posters, and flags. But there is also a $19.95 tape-playing machine that enables the candidate to carry his inspirational messages into the homes of voters over the telephone. There are Hertz rental cars equipped with bullhorn sound systems. And there is a $39.95 portable projector that flashes slogans, pictures, and plat-forms on anything from a living-room wall to the side of an office building. "Our job," the board chairman of CCI has said, "is to enable the low-budget candidate to get the most votes for his bucks."

> For well-heeled candidates, CCI will also arrange mass telephone campaigns at a cent and a half a call, state-wide voter polls (sample prices: $4,000 for Vermont, $9,000 for New York) and direct campaigns through Western Union Services or New York's big Reuben H. Donnelly Corporation. . . . "Whenever and wherever people elect people, we'll be there," says the CCI board chairman. "That's our market."[25]

How much American politics and parties will be affected by the coming of age of the mass media, technocracy, and the techniques of mass persuasion is

[25] *Newsweek*, April 29, 1968, p. 76. For a comprehensive study of the public relations man in politics, see Stanley Kelley, Jr., *Professional Public Relations and Political Power* (Baltimore: Johns Hopkins Press, 1956).

hard to say, though their impact is already sizable.[26] It is a good guess, say a variety of students of the media and politics, that the party organizations of the future will be stripped of most of their electoral functions, at least in major national campaigns. In their place will be a new politics dominated by image-makers and technical experts of all kinds—men who know what the public wants in its candidates and how to give it to them. Consider these facts and prognoses for an issueless, pseudo-politics:

> It is not surprising . . . that politicians and advertising men should have discovered one another. And, once they recognized that the citizen did not so much vote for a candidate as make a psychological purchase of him, not surprising that they began to work together. . . . Advertising agencies have tried openly to sell Presidents since 1952. When Dwight Eisenhower ran for re-election in 1956, the agency of Batton, Barton, Durstine and Osborn, which had been on a retainer throughout his first four years, accepted his campaign as a regular account. Leonard Hall, national Republican chairman, said: "You sell your candidates and your programs the way a business sells its products."[27]

> Day-by-day campaign reports spin on through regular newscasts and special reports. The candidates make their progress through engineered crowds, taking part in manufactured pseudo events, thrusting and parrying charges, projecting as much as they can, with the help of makeup and technology, the qualities of youth, experience, sincerity, popularity, alertness, wisdom, and vigor. And television follows them, hungry for material that is new and sensational. The new campaign strategists also generate films that are like syrupy documentaries: special profiles of candidates, homey, bathed in soft light, resonant with stirring music, creating personality images such as few mortals could emulate.[28]

> In all countries the party system has folded like the organization chart. Policies and issues are useless for election purposes, since they are too specialized and hot. The shaping of a candidate's integral image has taken the place of discussing conflicting points of view.[29]

> [Party] organizations find themselves increasingly dependent on management and consultant personnel, pollsters, and image-makers. The professional campaigners, instead of being the handmaidens of our major political parties, are

---

[26] Between 1964 and 1968 political expenditures for radio and television time for national campaigns increased by $24.6 million—from $34.6 million to $59.2 million. The total outlay was about $90 million in 1968 if related expenses, such as film-making and tape production, are included. *Congressional Quarterly Weekly Report*, May 1, 1970, p. 1184.

[27] Joe McGinniss, *The Selling of the President 1968*, p. 27. © 1969 by Joemac, Incorporated. Reprinted by permission of Trident Press/division of Simon & Schuster, Inc.

[28] Robert MacNeil, *The People Machine: The Influence of Television on American Politics* (New York: Harper & Row, Publishers, Inc., 1968), p. xvii.

[29] Marshall McLuhan, as quoted by McGinniss, *The Selling of the President 1968*, p. 28. © 1969 by Joemac, Incorporated. Reprinted by permission of Trident Press/division of Simon & Schuster, Inc.

independent factors in American elections. Parties turn to professional techni-
cians for advice on how to restructure their organizations, for information
about their clienteles, for fund-raising, and for recruiting new members. Candidates, winning nominations in primaries with the aid of professional campaigners rather than that of political parties, are increasingly independent of
partisan controls. The old politics does not rest well beside the new technology.[30]

No matter what happens, the national political parties of the future will no
longer be the same as in the past. Television had made the voter's home the
campaign amphitheater, and opinion surveys have made it his polling booth.
From this perspective, he has little regard for or need of a political party, at
least as we have known it, to show him how to release the lever on Election
Day.[31]

4. *The increasing nationalization of politics.* So unobtrusively has the
change taken place that a great many American citizens are doubtless unaware
of the extent to which sectional political alignments have been replaced by a
national political alignment. The Republican vote in the South in the 1952
presidential election was, it turns out, more than a straw in the wind. General
Dwight Eisenhower carried four southern states, narrowly lost several others,
made the Republican party respectable for many southern voters, and most
important laid the foundation for the development of a viable Republican
party throughout the South.

From the latter part of the nineteenth century until recently, the principal
obstacle to the emergence of a national politics was the hold of the Democratic
party on the South. Presidential, congressional, state, and local offices were
won, as a matter of course, by the Democratic party. But as Figure 13 and
Table 20 indicate, the Democratic grip on the southern states is no longer
firm. Taken as a whole, since 1952, southern states have been almost as likely
to vote Republican as to vote Democratic in presidential elections.[32] Probably of greater significance has been the growth of "congressional Republicanism" in the South. Table 20 attests to the striking gains made by the
Republican party in congressional elections from the early 1950s to the late
1960s. Democratic candidates for Congress in Arkansas, Florida, North
Carolina, Tennessee, and Virginia can no longer take elections for granted.
Even in the Deep South—Alabama, Georgia, Louisiana, Mississippi, and
South Carolina—Republican congressional candidacies have assumed new

[30] Dan Nimmo, *The Political Persuaders: The Techniques of Modern Election Campaigns* (Englewood Cliffs, N.J.: Prentice-Hall, 1970), p. 197.

[31] Harold Mendelsohn and Irving Crespi, *Polls, Television, and the New Politics*
(Scranton, Pa.: Chandler Publishing Company, 1970), pp. 310–311.

[32] The sharp drop in the Democratic vote in the 1968 presidential election, shown in
Figure 13, was due to the loss of votes to Wallace as well as to Nixon. Wallace won
the states of Alabama, Arkansas, Georgia, Louisiana, and Mississippi; Nixon carried
Florida, North Carolina, South Carolina, Tennessee, and Virginia; Humphrey won
only Texas.

Table 20

Republican Percentage of the Statewide Major Party
Vote for the U.S. House of Representatives, 1950–
1952, 1966–1968, Eleven Southern States*

| State | REPUBLICAN STATEWIDE PERCENTAGE | | | |
	1950	1952	1966	1968
Alabama	0.7	5.4	39.1	30.8
Arkansas	0.0	14.3	44.8	53.0
Florida	9.6	25.9	35.2	42.8
Georgia	0.0	0.0	34.4	20.5
Louisiana	0.0	8.7	18.2	18.8
Mississippi	0.0	2.5	21.2	7.5
North Carolina	30.0	32.2	47.1	45.4
South Carolina	0.0	2.0	29.3	32.8
Tennessee	30.3	29.8	50.0	51.1
Texas	9.5	1.3	16.6	28.1
Virginia	24.9	31.0	40.6	46.4

* Source of data: *The 1968 Elections* (Washington, D. C.: Republican National Committee, 1969), pp. 115–116.

life. Fewer and fewer southern Democratic candidates for Congress can expect to win election by default, no Republican opponent having been nominated to oppose them. There is a strong new breeze of Republicanism coursing through southern electorates. The insulation of southern politics from national political trends has not broken down completely, to be sure, but it has become remarkably porous.[33]

The movement from parochial to national politics has not been limited to the South. No matter what its history of party allegiance and voting, no state is wholly secure from incursions by the minority party. The vote in presidential elections now tends to be distributed more or less evenly throughout the country; fewer and fewer states register overwhelming victories for one or the other of the major parties. One-party political systems dwindle. "It is probably safe to say that in national and state-wide politics we are in the time of the most intense, evenly-spaced, two-party competitiveness of the last 100 years."[34]

[33] The best evidence that the "Solid South" has expired as a political entity will appear when Republicans contest vigorously with Democrats over local and state offices. During the 1960s, Republican gubernatorial candidates were elected in Florida and Arkansas. In 1970 the Democrats recaptured the state houses in Florida and Arkansas, but were defeated in Tennessee, when the first Republican in fifty years was elected to the governor's office. Republican gains at the state legislative level have been modest, except in Florida and Tennessee. Local offices continue to be dominated overwhelmingly by Democrats throughout the South.

[34] From Frank J. Sorauf, *Party Politics in America*, p. 48. Copyright © 1968 Little, Brown, and Company, Inc. Reprinted by permission.

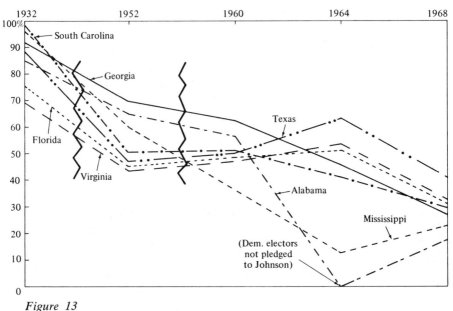

Figure 13
Democrats in Decline: Percentage of Vote Won
by Democratic Presidential Candidates, Selected
Southern States, 1932–1968

Source of data: U.S. Bureau of the Census, *Statistical Abstract of the United States* (Washington, D.C.). (Various editions.)

The sources for the growing nationalization of American politics are both numerous and varied. Social changes, rather than conscious party efforts to extend their spheres of influence, have provided the principal thrust for the new shape given to American party politics. Among the most important of these has been the emergence and extraordinary development of the mass media in political communications.[35] Through the electronic media, national political figures can be created virtually overnight, national issues can be carried to the most remote and inaccessible community, and new styles and trends can become a matter of common knowledge in a matter of days or

[35] One clue to how sharply political campaigns have changed emerges from these statistics: in sixty-two days of campaigning in 1968, Richard Nixon travelled 51,000 miles by jet aircraft and only 375 miles by train—all of the latter in a whistle-stop trip across Ohio. "It is quite probable that even the jet airplane will be displaced by television in the future. [As reported by a Gallup poll in late 1968], nearly half (44 percent) of the Americans sampled would not care if the entire campaign were conducted by radio and television only. Right now one of the prime reasons that Presidential campaigns go scooting about the country is simply to provide footage for both local and national television newscasts. . . ." Mendelsohn and Crespi, *Polls, Television, and the New Politics*, p. 301.

weeks. Insulation, old loyalties, and established patterns are difficult to maintain intact in the face of contemporary political communications. Consider these observations by Harvey Wheeler:

> Eisenhower was himself a newcomer to party politics. . . . He was heavily financed. He employed expensive and sophisticated mass media experts. "Madison Avenue" techniques were devised to project a predesigned "image." A new kind of electoral coalition was formed, composed largely of urban, white-collar people dissociated from the grass roots traditions of the agrarian past. His campaign cut across traditional party lines to orient itself about the personality of the candidate rather than the machine or the party. The new coalition of voter groups was socially and geographically mobile. The new politics required image manipulators rather than ballot box stuffers. The new organizations were ad hoc affairs created overnight by national cadres of advance men. The presidential primary overshadowed the party convention. This was to be the wave of the future. Television truly nationalized campaign communications and undermined the federal structure of the old machines. Party politics gave way to personality politics.[36]

For all their importance to the changes under way, the electronic media have not by themselves transformed the face of American politics. Changes in technology, the diversification of the economic bases of the states, the growth of an affluent society, the higher educational attainments of voters, the mobility of the population, the migration of black citizens to the North, the illumination of massive nationwide problems, the growth of vast urban conglomerations, and the assimilation of immigrant groups have all contributed to the erosion of internal barriers and parochialism and, consequently, to the strengthening of national political patterns. Whatever the complete explanation for this phenomenon, one thing is clear: the forces for the nationalization of politics are far more powerful today than the forces for localism and sectionalism.[37] A changing party system is the inevitable result.

5. *A new and growing concern over intraparty democracy.* A salutary result of the confusion, tumult, and divisiveness that characterized the 1968 Democratic National Convention in Chicago has been a sharp growth of interest in reforming the parties to make them internally democratic and more responsive to impulses for change. The drive for reform, particularly notice-

---

[36] Harvey Wheeler, "The End of the Two Party System," *Saturday Review*, November 2, 1968, p. 20. Copyright 1968, Saturday Review, Inc.

[37] The candidacy of George Wallace in 1968 does not impair this generalization. In one sense a southern candidate, Wallace nevertheless gained a place on the ballot everywhere except the District of Columbia, campaigned throughout the nation, and for a third-party candidate, won a surprising number of popular votes in the North—over 8 percent in the nonsouthern states as a whole. Wallace's campaign was addressed to the interests, frustrations, and anxieties of some people in all parts of the country, obviously not to southern voters alone. The difference between the 1948 Dixiecrat campaign and the 1968 Wallace movement was, among other things, the difference between sectional politics and national politics.

able in the Democratic party, centers on the presidential nominating process. To study problems of party reform, the 1968 Democratic Convention authorized the formation of two commissions. The first, the Commission on Party Structure and Delegate Selection, was charged with the responsibility for developing guidelines for revisions in the delegate selection process in order to assure broad citizen participation and to make the party representative of grass-roots sentiment. The second, the Rules Commission, was formed to study and develop proposals for the reform of the national nominating convention and the reform of the rules and structure of the Democratic National Committee.

The report of the Commission on Party Structure and Delegate Selection is especially instructive.[38] Commenting on the overall process by which delegates were selected to the 1968 Convention, the Commission observed that "meaningful participation of Democratic voters in the choice of their presidential nominee was often difficult or costly, sometimes completely illusory, and, in not a few instances, impossible." For example, the Commission found that: (1) in nearly half the states rules governing the selection process were either nonexistent or inadequate, "leaving the entire process to the discretion of a handful of party leaders;" (2) over one-third of the Convention delegates had, in effect, been chosen prior to 1968—well before all the possible presidential candidates were known and before President Johnson had withdrawn from the race; (3) "the imposition of the unit rule from the first to the final stage of the nominating process, the enforcement of binding instructions on delegates, and favorite-son candidacies were all devices used to force Democrats to vote against their stated presidential preferences;" (4) in primary, convention, and committee delegate selection systems, "majorities used their numerical superiority to deny delegate representation to the supporters of minority presidential candidates;" (5) procedural irregularities, such as secret caucuses, closed slate-making, and proxy voting, were common in party conventions from the precinct to the state level; (6) the costs of participating in the delegate selection process, such as filing fees for entering primaries, were often excessive; and (7) certain population groups—in particular blacks, women, and youth—were substantially underrepresented among the delegates.

To combat the inequitable practices and arrangements utilized by state and local parties, the Commission adopted a series of guidelines to regulate the selection of delegates for future conventions. Designed to permit all Democratic voters a "full, meaningful, and timely" opportunity to take part in the presidential nominating process, the guidelines set forth an extensive array of

[38] The findings and recommendations of this Commission, discussed in this and the following four paragraphs, may be found in the publication, *Mandate for Reform* (Washington, D.C.: Commission on Party Structure and Delegate Selection, Democratic National Committee, 1970).

reforms to be implemented by state parties (and where appropriate, by state legislatures).

The initial step required of state Democratic parties is that they adopt a comprehensive set of rules governing the delegate selection process to which all rank-and-file Democrats would have access. These rules should not only make clear how all party members can participate in the process but also be designed in such a way as to facilitate their "maximum participation." In addition, certain procedural safeguards are required. Proxy voting, the use of the unit rule, and the practice of instructing delegates are forbidden. Party committee meetings are to require a quorum of not less than 40 percent of the members. Mandatory assessments of convention delegates is prohibited. Adequate public notice of all party meetings called to consider delegate selection is required as are rules to provide for uniform times and dates of meetings.

The Commission enjoined state parties to seek a broad base of support. Standards eliminating all forms of discrimination against the participation of minority group members in the delegate selection process are to be adopted. Moreover, to overcome the effects of past discrimination, each state is expected to include in its delegation blacks, women, and young people in numbers roughly proportionate to their presence in the state population.

A number of specific requirements for delegate selection were adopted by the Commission. For example, provisions must be made for selection of delegates in a "timely manner" (within the calendar year in which the Convention is held), for selection of alternates in the same manner as delegates, for apportionment of delegates within the state on the basis of a formula that gives equal weight to population and to Democratic strength, for selection of at least 75 percent of the delegates at congressional district or small unit levels (in states using the convention system), and for selection of no more than 10 percent of the total delegation by the state committee.

How fully state Democratic parties will comply with the guidelines of the Commission remains to be seen. Although some states quickly brought their delegate selection systems into harmony with the Commission's standards, others have temporized on the matter. In many states, legislative as well as party action is required to make changes; where statutory changes are necessary, reform has been difficult to bring about. Here and there reform bills have been blocked by Republican legislators. Elsewhere Democratic legislative leaders have made little effort to pass reform bills and then proceeded to place the blame on the Republicans. It is probable that any state party that ignores or makes little effort to comply with the Commission's guidelines will be challenged over the seating of its delegates to the convention.[39]

[39] Ken Bode, "Democratic Party Reform," *New Republic*, July 10, 1971, pp. 19–23.

The proposals of the other reform unit of the Democratic party, the Rules Commission, reflect a similar concern over democratization of the party system. Among other things, its recommendations call for open meetings of the major convention committees, selection of key committee chairmen by the convention members themselves (rather than by the party's national chairman), and apportionment of convention delegates to the states on a basis that awards larger states (with larger Democratic votes) a greater measure of representation.

The thrust of the current efforts to reform the Democratic party is unmistakable. Party structures and processes are to be made opener, more representative, and more responsive to rank-and-file members. This, in fact, was one of the major objectives the Committee on Political Parties had in mind in its report, *Toward a More Responsible Two-Party System.* "In a party system organized on democratic lines and with a national point of view," the *Report* contends, "cohesion springs naturally from willingness to support aims which the member himself has helped to shape and has come to accept."[40]

The issue of intraparty democracy is likely to be a persistent problem for the parties during the decade of the 1970s. Broadly speaking, what has happened is that the philosophy of "one man–one vote," now dominant for the election of American legislators, has been extended to the party system. Thus far only the Democratic party has grappled seriously with the problem. The Republican party, of course, also has its share of unrepresentative practices— practices that tend to invest some party members with vastly more influence than others. It would be surprising indeed if the challenge of reform were not extended to it.

The Prospects

The American party system has been shaped more by custom and environment than by intent. The changes that come to it, as a result, come slowly. Indeed, in broad contour, the parties of today resemble closely those of previous generations. For as long as any of us can remember, the major parties have been loose and disorderly coalitions, heavily decentralized, lacking in unity and discipline, preoccupied with winning office, and no more than erratically "responsible" for the conduct of government and the formation of public policy. There is, of course, another side to them. They have performed at least as well as the parties of other democratic nations—and perhaps far

[40] Committee on Political Parties of the American Political Science Association, *Toward a More Responsible Two-Party System,* p. 66.

better. Democratic politics requires the maintainence of a predictable legal system; institutionalized arrangements for popular control of government and the mobilization of majorities; methods and arenas for the illumination, crystallization, and reconciliation of conflict; and means for endowing both leaders and policies with legitimacy. To each of these requirements the parties have contributed steadily and often in major ways.[41]

It is a truism of American politics that it is invariably difficult to cut free from familiar institutions. Old practices die hard. Conventional arrangements hang on and on. Change arrives incrementally and unnoticed. Not only are most Americans habituated to the parties as they are but the parties themselves are accustomed to the environment in which they function. It would seem that prospects for the development of a system of responsible parties are thin at best. But the matter deserves a closer look.

It seems clear that on most counts the parties have lost ground in recent years. The electoral party organizations undoubtedly have been weakened. Their control over the nominating process, once a virtual monopoly, has gradually slipped away. Primary battles for major offices appear to occur more and more frequently. So-called independent candidates seem to be both more numerous and more successful than in the past. A gradual loosening of the electorate's ties to the parties is also evident. There are more people who regard themselves as independents today than ever before—almost as many, in fact, as those who describe themselves as Republicans. The power of local party bosses probably never has been less formidable than it is today. The media, public relations consultants, and campaign management firms are now as much a part of political campaigns as the party organizations themselves— at least when important offices are at stake. In sum, in the recruitment-campaign-election stages of the political process, American parties gradually have lost power. They compete within the political process but do not dominate it. A great deal of contemporary politics, in fact, lies outside the parties and beyond their control.

At another level of analysis, however, there are signs that bode well for the party system. The state of flux that now characterizes the parties carries signs of health as well as of malaise. No one can predict confidently the shape of the parties in the decades to come. However, the growing nationalization of politics, marked particularly by an expansion of competition, is unmistakable. Other changes, congruent with this development, may follow in

---

[41] To explore the literature that defends the American party system, see in particular Herbert Agar, *The Price of Union*; Pendleton Herring, *The Politics of Democracy* (New York: Norton, 1940); Arthur N. Holcombe, *Our More Perfect Union* (Cambridge, Mass.: Harvard University Press, 1950); and Edward C. Banfield, "In Defense of the American Party System," in Robert A. Goldwin (ed.), *Political Parties, U.S.A.* (Chicago: Rand McNally, 1964), pp. 21–39.

its wake. Among the most likely are (1) a growth in importance of national party organizations over state and local party organizations; (2) a more frequent party alternation in power as the parties become more evenly matched throughout the country; (3) a decline in the number of states and voters who, insulated by one-party systems, will be able to elude the great issues that course through the nation; (4) the development of majorities in one part of the country that resemble those in other parts of the country, contributing to the formation of a national electorate and a national majority; (5) an extension of the range of choice open to electorates as future political agendas come to be dominated by national rather than sectional or parochial issues; (6) a growth in the representativeness and responsiveness of the nation's political institutions, particularly Congress and the national conventions; (7) and a new interest in the reform of the parties themselves as ancient barriers to change erode.

All things considered, the prospects for the development of a full-blown, responsible party system, along the lines described at the outset of this chapter, are anything but bright. Too many obstacles—constitutional, political, and otherwise—stand in the way. But this is not to say that responsible party performance in government is unattainable. The way in which parties govern is far from dependent upon the strength and vitality of the electoral party organizations or upon the way in which men and women are elected to office. The party-in-the-government, it is worth remembering, is both different from the party-in-the-electorate and largely independent of it.

The essence of a responsible party system is not to be found in party councils, closed primaries, representative national conventions, or even in intraparty democracy—important as these appear. Rather, the key idea is represented in party responsibility for a program of public policy. Such responsibility requires, in the first place, a strong measure of internal cohesion within the party-in-the-government in order to adopt its program and, in the second place, an electorate sufficiently sensitive to party accomplishments and failures that it can hold the parties accountable for their records, particularly in the case of the party in power. At times neither requirement can be met to any degree. When the executive and legislative branches are controlled by different parties, for example, party responsibility goes by the boards. Nevertheless, there are occasions when American political institutions function in a manner largely consonant with the party responsibility model.

A responsible party system at the national level demands a particular kind of Congress—one in which power is centralized rather than dispersed. Over long stretches of time Congress has not been organized in such a way as to permit the parties, *qua* parties, to govern. The seniority system, the independence of committees and their chairmen, the filibuster, the weaknesses present in elected party positions and agencies, and the unrepresentativeness of Congress itself have made it difficult for party majorities to assert themselves and to act in the name of the party.[42]

Every so often, however, the congressional party comes fully alive. Consider the first session of the 89th Congress (1965)—"the most dramatic illustration in a generation of the capacity of the President and the Congress to work together on important issues of public policy":

> In part a mopping up operation on an agenda fashioned at least in spirit by the New Deal, the work of the 89th Congress cut new paths through the frontier of qualitative issues: a beautification bill, a bill to create federal support for the arts and humanities, vast increases in federal aid to education. . . . [The] policy leadership and the legislative skill of President Johnson found a ready and supportive response from a strengthened partisan leadership and a substantial, presidentially oriented Democratic majority in both houses. A decade of incremental structural changes in the locus of power in both houses eased the President's task of consent-building and legislative implementation.
>
> Yet Congress was far from being just a rubber stamp. On some issues the President met resounding defeat. On many issues, presidential recommendations were modified by excisions or additions—reflecting the power of particular committee chairmen, group interests, and bureaucratic pressures at odds with presidential perspectives.
>
> [The lessons of the 89th Congress] proved that vigorous presidential leadership and sizable partisan majorities in both houses of the same partisan persuasion as the President, could act in reasonable consonance, and with dispatch, in fashioning creative answers to major problems. The nation's voters could pin responsibility upon a national party for the legislative output. If that partisan majority erred in judgment, it could at least be held accountable in ensuing congressional and presidential elections.[43]

---

[42] These barriers to party majority-building have become increasingly vulnerable. For example, it appears certain that seniority gradually will become less significant as a support for the power of southern Democrats. Two reasons explain this: the growing threat of Republican candidates to congressional seats long held by southern Democrats and the sharp increase in the number of Democratic safe seats in northern states—a condition that inevitably will produce substantial seniority and, accordingly, committee chairmanships. On the second point, see an article by Raymond E. Wolfinger and Joan Heifetz, "Safe Seats, Seniority, and Power in Congress," *American Political Science Review*, LIX (June 1965), especially p. 347. For a wide-ranging analysis of the emergence and consolidation of the seniority system, see Nelson W. Polsby, Miriam Gallaher, and Barry S. Rundquist, "The Growth of the Seniority System in the U.S. House of Representatives," *American Political Science Review*, LXIII (September 1969), pp. 787–807.

[43] Stephen K. Bailey, *Congress in the Seventies* (New York: St. Martin's Press, 1970), pp. 102–103. Among the other major accomplishments of the first session of the 89th Congress were the passage of bills to provide for medical care for the aged under Social Security, aid to depressed areas, the protection of voting rights, federal scholarships, the Teacher Corps, immigration reform, and a variety of programs to launch the war on poverty.

The chances are that there will be future Congresses like "the fabulous 89th"—the label bestowed on it by President Johnson. No one, of course, should expect them to be strung together, one following another. The conditions must be right: a large partisan majority, more or less ideologically unified, and a vigorous President are essential. A long policy agenda may also be required. In any case, the point not to be missed is that, under the right circumstances, the deadlocks in American politics can be broken and the political system can function vigorously and with a high degree of cooperation between the branches of government. "Party responsibility" can thrive even if unrecognized and unlabeled. The evidence of the 89th Congress suggests that the first requirement for government be responsible parties—a fairly high degree of internal party agreement on policy—can, at least occasionally, be met.

The second requirement—an electorate attuned to party performance in government—is a much different matter. The total system of responsible parties breaks down at precisely this point:

> What the public knows about the legislative records of the parties and of individual congressional candidates is a principal reason for the departure of American practice from an idealized conception of party government. . . . The electorate sees very little altogether of what goes on in the national legislature. Few judgments of legislative performance are associated with the parties, and much of the public is unaware even of which party has control of Congress. . . . Many of those who have commented on the lack of party discipline in Congress have assumed that the Congressman votes against his party because he is forced to by the demands of one of several hundred constituencies of a superlatively heterogeneous nation. In some cases, the Representative may subvert the proposals of his party because his constituency demands it. But a more reasonable interpretation over a broader range of issues is that the Congressman fails to see these proposals as part of a program on which the party—and he himself—will be judged at the polls, because he knows the constituency isn't looking.[44]

Experiments with forms of party responsibility, like fashion, will perhaps always possess a probationary quality—tried, neglected, forgotten, and rediscovered. The tone and mood of such a system will doubtless appear on occasion, but without the public either anticipating it or recognizing it when it arrives. More generally, however, the party system is likely to resemble, at least in broad lines, the model to which we are adjusted and inured: the parties situated precariously atop the political process, threatened and thwarted by a variety of competitors, uncomfortably coalitional, active in fits and starts and often in hiding, beset by factional rifts, frustrated by the

---

[44] Donald E. Stokes and Warren E. Miller, "Party Government and the Saliency of Congress," Angus Campbell, et al., (eds), *Elections and the Political Order*, pp. 209–211.

growing independence of voters, and moderately irresponsible. From the vantage point of both outsiders and insiders, the party system ordinarily will appear, to the extent that it registers at all, in disarray. And indeed it is in disarray—more so than at any time in the last century—but not to a point that either promises or insures its enfeeblement and disintegration.[45]

[45] For an unusually provocative and instructive study of the decline of the parties in the electorate, see Walter Dean Burnham, *Critical Elections and the Mainsprings of American Politics*. Burnham writes: "The pattern of change in recent years seems fairly clear. The political parties are progressively losing their hold upon the electorate. A new breed of independent seems to be emerging as well—a person with a better-than-average education, making a better-than-average income in a better-than-average occupation, and, very possibly, a person whose political cognitions and awareness keep him from making identifications with either old party. The losses the two parties, particularly the Democrats, have suffered in this decade have largely been concentrated among precisely those strata in the population most likely to act through and in the political system out of proportion to their numbers. This may point toward the progressive dissolution of the parties as action intermediaries in electoral choice and other politically relevant acts. It may also be indicative of the production of a mass base for independent political movements of ideological tone and considerable long-term staying power." Quotation drawn from pp. 130–131.

Index

White, Theodore H., 74
Wilson, James Q., 15, 16
Wilson, Woodrow, 98
Wisconsin, electorate, 6–8
    voluntary party associations, 15
Wofford, Harris, 74

Wolfe, Arthur G., 97, 148
Wolfinger, Raymond E., 161

Yarborough, Ralph W., 45

Zeigler, Harmon, 73